Elijah

Steps to a Life of Power

Bob Saffrin

CONTENTS

ACKNOWLEDGMENTS

As I think about those who helped me get to the place where I am, writing and publishing books, I am overwhelmed by the many who have encouraged me along the path. I think of Sam Saffrin, a dad who convinced me that I could do anything I set my mind to, before I was old enough to doubt him. I think of family and the many Christian friends who have encouraged me and urged me to write.

Specifically for "Elijah" I want to thank Lori Moen, Michaela Moen, Barb Saffrin, Joy Christiansen, and Julie Saffrin for editing the text and Joy Christiansen for the terrific cover design. Mostly I want to thank the Holy Spirit for inspiring the Biblical story of Elijah and for helping me understand the insights showing how Elijah's story applies to us today.

"Many of the people of Israel will he bring back to the Lord their God. And he will go on before the Lord, in the spirit and power of Elijah, to turn the hearts of the fathers to their children and the disobedient to the wisdom of the righteous — to make ready a people prepared for the Lord."
Luke 1:16-17

INTRODUCTION

Elijah (Yahweh is my strength)

When I first started going to India, my love for adventure drew me to the country more than did my passion for souls. Eventually, the passion for souls came, though, when I sensed the spiritual darkness of the place and began to see the spiritual hunger and desperation of the beautiful people of India.

I started going to the rural state of Andhra Pradesh in 2002. Each year I returned for several weeks, going with just an interpreter into the country's interior, hanging out in poor, remote villages, making friends, and talking to people about Jesus, the one true

God. After several of these "hanging out" trips, talking to a few people at a time, the state church leadership convinced me to hold open-air Gospel festival meetings so I could speak to more people about the God of love in a more efficient way. And so, in March of 2006, I found myself on a stage in Tanguturu, a remote village in south India, sitting on a platform just a few miles from the Bay of Bengal, waiting to speak to more than one thousand people who had gathered to hear what this strange-looking foreigner had to say.

Sitting next to me was a new friend whom I had just met. Boneface, a Nigerian, had come to India with a similar call to adventure. He was a man of prayer, drawn to the sick and infirm; he would sometimes pray all night for someone's healing. That first night in Tanguturu, I asked him to sit with me on the platform. As we sat there, I looked at the crowd of excited and anticipating faces and was suddenly overcome with a complete sense of unworthiness. I thought, why would God send me here? Why had God chosen me, this little teacher/preacher with very little giftings, no voice of authority, and no big-haired evangelist look? Uncertainty and fear gripped me. This was the largest crowd I had ever spoken to and I felt totally inadequate. I would have jumped off that stage and run, but where does one run to when in Tanguturu?

As the final song was sung before I was to be introduced, I leaned to Boneface and out of fear and desperation blurted, "I don't know why I am here. I don't know why God would send me here to speak to these people, Why me?" Without hesitation, and with a big grin, Boneface turned to me and said, "You are here because the donkey was busy tonight." He was making a not-so-veiled reference to the prophet Balaam's talking donkey in the Old Testament.

I got the message. God uses anything or anyone He chooses.

When Jesus approached Jerusalem for the last time, riding on a donkey, the Israelites began to shout, cheer, and praise God. When the religious leaders tried to hush the people and told Jesus to rebuke them, He said, "I tell you...if they keep quiet, the stones will cry out"(Luke 19:40).

Boniface's point was clear. God had spoken to me through my new friend; I had learned a lesson that I would not forget. God uses what He chooses. He can speak through a donkey, a rock, or even an inadequate and scared little Jewish boy.

Ten years later, the crowds in India have grown to over ten thousand. The feelings of inadequacy are still there, but I have witnessed God do some amazing things with my inability.

This may surprise you, but Elijah, the towering, mighty prophet of Israel, the man who spoke for God, Israel's prophet of prophets, was also just an inadequate, scared little Jewish boy. Nothing about him made him great, not his rugged good looks, his great intellect or his heroic courage. On his own, he was flawed, petty and a coward. The Bible says that he was a person "just like us." Why then, would we look at Elijah's life and hold it up as an example of living a life of power? Precisely because he was just like you and me. Today, centuries later, religious leaders herald Elijah as the Martin Luther of old-time Israel, crediting him with turning the hearts of the people from the corrupt state-sponsored religion back to the worship of the one true God.

If Elijah was a person no different than you and me, and if he did it, then why can't we? Is it possible that God can use us to turn the hearts of the people of our generation back to God?

Could it be that Elijah's mission is our mission, "...to make ready a people prepared for the Lord" (Luke 1:17). -- Yes! That's right my friend. God's mission for us is to prepare the people of this generation for the coming of the Lord. Go ahead, shiver a little; shake in your boots. You say, "Come on Bob! Me, prepare the way for the Lord, with my limitations! With my sin! I don't even know if I'll make it through the week. I am consumed with just surviving a culture that presses in from every side. Even if I had the time and energy, I don't have the abilities to be that kind of person? Sorry, Bob, you've got the wrong person." Welcome to Elijah's world. He had nothing within himself that would make him fit for the mission that God gave him. How then was he able to become Israel's prophet? The answer to that question is the reason for this book. How was a simple man, a man no different than you and me, able to be so mightily used by God? How did he become the huge man of power and strength that defeated evil in his day? When we find the answer to that question, we will be on the path to the journey that God has for each of us. My prayer for you is that the story of Elijah will change your life as it has mine.

Life Lesson

God isn't looking for great people, he's looking for available people (Elijah was a man "just like us").

Consider and discuss: How available are you to God? God is such a respecter of our free will that he will rarely burst in on us in the middle of us doing our thing. We must seek him. He usually doesn't barge in on our consciousness with brash overtures of wind or earthquakes, but with a quiet whisper.

Are you listening? Do you get quiet enough to hear God speak? Are you intentional about seeking his dream for your life? God only uses those people who are available to him. How available are you? What are the things in your life that hold you back from following God to great adventures? Elijah was constantly aware of God's presence.

Make a list of the ways you can become more aware of His daily presence.

CHAPTER 1

Living the Dream

Why a book about Elijah? Wasn't he just one of those dusty Old Testament prophets? Born around 900 BC, his life was very important to the Israelites three thousand years ago, but is there some modern significance to the man? After all these centuries, how can Elijah's story possibly make a difference to your story or mine? He was well known in his own time and even today. Most people know of the Old Testament prophet Elijah. More than one thousand years after he lived he was mentioned twenty-eight times by the various authors of the New Testament books, and along with Moses, he actually appeared in New Testament times. He must have been an imposing personality.

Shortly before his crucifixion Jesus went up on a mountain to pray. As he was praying, two men, Elijah and Moses, appeared and talked with Jesus. Luke 9 says that Elijah and Moses appeared in "glorious splendor."

In addition, a special link existed between the lives of Elijah and John the Baptist.

> And he [John the Baptist] will go on before the Lord, in the spirit and power of Elijah, to turn the hearts of the fathers to their children and the disobedient to the wisdom of the righteous — to make ready a people prepared for the Lord.
>
> (Luke 1:17)

That last little phrase, "to make ready a people prepared for the Lord," accurately identifies God's vision for both men. How we need men and women today who are called to prepare and strengthen God's people.

The Old Testament book of Malachi predicts the return of Elijah:

> See, I will send you the prophet Elijah before that great and dreadful day of the Lord comes. He will turn the hearts of the fathers to their children, and the hearts of the children to their fathers.

> (Mal. 4:5-6)

Because of that prediction, some thought Elijah would come to rescue Jesus as he hung on the cross -

> And at the ninth hour Jesus cried out in a loud voice, "Eloi, Eloi, lama sabachthani?" - which means, "My God, my God, why have you forsaken me?" When some of those standing near heard this, they said, "Listen, he's calling Elijah." One man ran, filled a sponge with wine vinegar, put it on a stick, and offered it to Jesus to drink. "Now leave him alone. Let's see if Elijah comes to take him down," he said.

> (Mark 15:34-36)

In fact, the New Testament speaks of Elijah more than any other Old Testament prophet. Do you get the idea that Elijah was somebody special?

Now let's get personal. God has a call on your life. God is a God of dreams and he created you to fulfill a dream. He has a purpose for you. In my last book, "Moses - Steps to a Life of Faith," we saw that in order for God to fulfill his dream in us we have to first believe him and trust him for that dream. Okay, so God has a call on your life. The question is do you have the time, energy and ability to respond to God's call. Think about your day-to-day schedule. Do you even have the energy to discover his call, let alone live it?

We all struggle with busyness. We feel stretched in every direction with all the demands on our time. Have you ever said, "I'm only one person?" Do you ever feel this way? With the pressures of just daily living, how can we possibly find time to respond to God's mission? What can we possibly do for God when just "living" takes all of our time? What is needed? Do we need more than twenty-four hours in a day? Do we need more than seven days a week? I hope not, because I'm pretty sure 24/7 is all we're going to get. The answer, of course, is not that we need more time. We have plenty of time. Energy and focus is what we lack. What we really need is more POWER! Don't you think that if God has a dream for your life and if he intends to live out that dream in you, that he will also give you the power needed to energize that dream?

God has given us his Holy Spirit as a dynamo to charge up our lives and give us what we need to live the dream. All we need to do is learn how to tap into and live in that power.

I fear the church today has largely missed what it means to live in the power of the Holy Spirit. Some of us are just trying to drag ourselves through the week and somehow hang on until Friday. Then there are others who really believe they have received the power of the Holy Spirit. That is wonderful. I praise the Lord for brothers and sisters who are truly living in the power of the Holy Spirit, but we have to remember that the test of God's power in our lives is not measured in giftedness or manifestations. The test of God's power in our lives is measured by the lives that are changed as we rub shoulders with others. Elijah's life is not measured by his ability to call fire from heaven, but rather by the hearts of the Israelites turned back to the worship of Jehovah. In the upper room at Pentecost, as Jesus' disciples were praying, they asked for power to proclaim the Gospel. The mighty rushing wind and the tongues of fire were pretty amazing, but the real measure of power was the three-thousand souls that were saved that day.

Think about this: If you were able to tap into enough power, if you had enough physical, emotional, mental, and spiritual vitality, how much could you accomplish for the Kingdom of God in your life? Let me ask the question another way. How much could God do through your life if He had it at his disposal? How much could one man (or woman) do in his lifetime if he was willing to be a conduit of God's power to a lost and dying world? Would there be any limit to the possible usefulness of such a life?

On the one hand, we have the fullness and completeness of God. In him we have total purity and total love. On the other hand, we have the complete neediness of man, - guilty, weak, unable to love or be loved. All that is needed is a channel of communication between the two, an open channel to carry the fullness of God to the emptiness of man. We need a channel of power to enable the unlovely and unloving to receive and pass on the love of the Creator.

God has ordained the church to be that channel, and friends, you and I are the church. The church is not that building down the street where services are held. The "church" is wherever two or more gather to share Christ together. How many of us does God need to get the job done? The story of Elijah tells us how God used one man, to channel his love and power to a lost and depraved world. Could God save the lost and depraved world we live in with just one person who was completely at his disposal? Could that one person be you?

Life Lesson

How can I find the time and energy to be God's person when I'm already stretched to the limit?

Consider and discuss: Think about your typical day. What fills it? How much of what you do will count for eternity or even has current value?

Do you believe that God has a dream and a purpose for your life? If he does, do you believe that if you submit to God he will so order your days to ensure that his dream for you will fit into your schedule. If you can't find the time, do you think the problem is that God hasn't given you enough time or that somehow you are not spending it the way he has ordained?

Make a list of your daily activities. What about your daily activity exemplifies that you are walking in the power of the Spirit?

CHAPTER 2

The setting for Elijah's story

For over one hundred years in Israel the tide had been running against the truth of God. Idolatry had become the norm. Worship had degenerated from Jeroboam's calves to the worship of Baal, the storm god, and Ashtoreth, the goddess of fertility. They had a formal worship system, maintained by an organization of crooked priests who had settled in on the nation of Israel like a fungus. The Baal and Ashtoreth worship was supported by a government that consisted of a weak King Ahab and his not-so-weak but unscrupulous wife,

Jezebel. Jehovah's altars had all been destroyed and all of the true prophets had either been killed or were in hiding.

The lamp of truth had been kicked over in Israel and there was only a tiny spark where once the light of true faith had shone brightly.

Israel's fall started with King Solomon. God had warned Israel to not intermarry with certain other nations or their hearts would be turned to other gods. In spite of God's warning Solomon had seven hundred wives and three hundred concubines, mostly from those foreign nations. Just as God had predicted, Solomon's wives corrupted him and he began to worship their false gods. His heart was no longer devoted to only the Lord God. King Solomon, who in his younger years was known as the wisest of men, became foolish in his later years and did evil in the eyes of God.

> The Lord became angry with Solomon because his heart had turned away from the Lord, the God of Israel, who had appeared to him twice. Although he had forbidden Solomon to follow other gods,

> Solomon did not keep the Lord's
> command.

(1 Kings 11:9-10)

It was a sad epitaph on the life of a man who had prayed for wisdom that he might lead his people. Eventually, the Lord took the nation of Israel away from Solomon:

> Now Jeroboam was a man of standing, and when Solomon saw how well the young man did his work, he put him in charge of the whole labor force of the house of Joseph. About that time Jeroboam was going out of Jerusalem, and Ahijah the prophet of Shiloh met him on the way, wearing a new cloak. The two of them were alone out in the country, and Ahijah took hold of the new cloak he was wearing and tore it into twelve pieces. Then he said to Jeroboam, "Take ten pieces for yourself, for this is what the Lord, the God of Israel, says: See, I am going to tear the kingdom out of Solomon's hand and give you ten tribes".

(1 Kings 11:28-31)

And so, the Jewish nation was split into the northern kingdom of Israel and the southern kingdom of Judah. Jeroboam became king of the ten northern tribes and only the tribes of Judah and Benjamin remained loyal to Rehoboam, Solomon's son. But Jeroboam had a problem. He was the king of the ten northern tribes but the people still went to Jerusalem in the south to worship Jehovah and bring their sacrifices. He was afraid that eventually they would become loyal to the southern kingdom, kill him, and give their allegiance to Rehoboam, king of Judah. To solve this problem, he made them two golden calves to worship. He said to the people: "It is too much for you to go up to Jerusalem. Here are your gods, O Israel, who brought you up out of Egypt" (1 Kings 12:28).

"Here are your gods, O Israel, who brought you up out of Egypt." This is the kind of stuff that really makes God mad! Jeroboam didn't need to try to consolidate his power. God had given him the northern tribes; men wouldn't be able to take them away from him. Jeroboam's problem was that he feared people more than he trusted God. Think about those areas of your life where you are motivated by your fear of what others will think of you. I wonder how many

God-given dreams have been thwarted by fear of what others may think.

And so, the northern tribes fell away from their worship of the one true God to worship the golden idols of Jeroboam. Five kings ruled in Israel after Jeroboam until eventually King Ahab sat on the throne, ruling with his wife, Jezebel. The Bible says that King Ahab did more evil in the eyes of the Lord than any other king before him:

> Ahab also made an Asherah pole and did more to provoke the Lord, the God of Israel, to anger than did all the kings of Israel before him.

> (1 Kings 16:31-33)

Things were in a sorry state in Israel. All the prophets of God were either dead or in hiding. Of the millions of Israelites, there were only seven thousand left who had not worshipped Baal. How would you compare those days to ours? Where were the believers back then? Where was the power of the Holy Spirit in the land to convict men of sin and draw them to God? Where is it today? I believe that we live in a day that is very much like Elijah's day. I think God is looking for men and women like Elijah to help turn the hearts of today's people back to God. He is not looking for people with great abilities; he is looking for those who will simply be available to him.

Life Lesson

_____

Leaving a legacy...” What do you want on your tombstone?”

Consider and discuss: The life we live has a sum total that adds up to something. What does yours add up to so far? What will people say about you when your story ends? Will you make a difference?

When people talk about the spirit of Elijah, they say that he had a purpose - to turn the hearts of the people back to the worship of the one true God; that he had a mission, “to make ready a people prepared for the Lord.”

Has God given you a purpose, a mission? God has a plan for everyone. What are you doing to discover his plan for you?

Matthew 28:19-20

Go therefore and make disciples of all the nations, baptizing them in the name of the Father and the Son and the Holy Spirit

teaching them to observe all that I commanded you; and lo, I am with you always, even to the end of the age.

CHAPTER 3

Enter Elijah!

It was on this scene that Elijah enters the picture. Now we need to be careful to remember that Elijah wasn't someone with special abilities. He was a common man, a highlander from the hills of Jordan. He was unkempt, unpolished, and uneducated. He was weak where you and I are weak, tempted where we are tempted. Elijah wasn't great, but God was able to do great things using Elijah as a channel of his power. Elijah wasn't great, but the connection between him and God was great.

God's power was able to flow through him. Jehovah was his source.

As we look at the story of Elijah, let's remember that our quest is to discover God and how we can make that kind of a connection with him. As soon as Elijah entered the scene, the tide began to turn in Israel. The progress of idolatry was checked. Jehovah was again given his place as the God of the Israelites. Truth reigned again in Israel and its effect felt for many generations.

The secret to Elijah's power was that he was filled with the Holy Spirit.

It was a privilege for a select few in his day. Today the Holy Spirit is not only available to us all but he is a requirement for success as a Christian. If you know Jesus as your Savior then the Holy Spirit lives in you. But there are many Christians who do not live lives of joy and power. When you are "saved", God lives in you, but to be "filled" with the Holy Spirit is to give control of your life to God. The New Testament tells us: "Do not get drunk on wine, which leads to debauchery, instead, be filled with the

Spirit" (Eph. 5:18). "Be filled"...it's an imperative.

The story begins!

The first time we hear of the prophet Elijah is in 1 Kings where he bursts in on the scene un-announced:

> Now Elijah the Tishbite, from Tishbe in Gilead, said to Ahab, "As the Lord, the God of Israel, lives, whom I serve, there will be neither dew nor rain in the next few years except at my word."

(1 Kings 17:1)

The story begins with the word "Now" as translated by the New International Version of the Bible. Literally, the rendering should be "And then." This is significant because it indicates that the preceding chapters are not the end of the story. The nation of Israel had fallen hopelessly into idolatry. Everyone thought the worship of Jehovah would never again acquire its lost prestige and power. Ahab thought so, Jezebel thought so, and the false prophets thought so. Sadly, the hidden and frightened remnant of true disciples thought so. But they all made an unfortunate omission in their assessment of the situation. They had forgotten Jehovah himself who would yet have something to say about the state of things. God was ready to add a few chapters before the story was finished.

Often, when people have done their worst and finished, it is time for God to begin. And when God begins, he is likely in one stroke of the pen to undo all that has been done without him, and to write new pages of human history as a lesson for all who will come after.

The words "And then" are ominous words to God's enemies, but they are full of hope and promise to his friends. Whatever you are going through today, whatever crisis turn your life has taken, whatever failure and disappointment plagues you, God is waiting in the wings of your situation ready to come in and wipe it all away and re-write your story with an "And then!" This is good news. It doesn't matter how bad things get; God is never at a loss.

> And I tell you that you are Peter, and on this rock I will build my church, and the gates of Hades will not overcome it.

(Matt. 16:18)

Just when things seem their worst, God will be preparing some weak man or woman to send forth in his power and in the moment of greatest need. God loves to come in like the cavalry at the last minute after all our striving and struggling has failed, and he loves to manifest his power in our weakness.

> From the west, men will fear the name of the Lord, and from the rising of the sun, they will revere his glory; for he will come like a pent-up flood that the breath of the Lord drives along.

(Isa. 59:19)

God loves to take the weakest person he can find, and use that person to accomplish his work. In 1st Corinthians, the Apostle Paul tells us that God chose the foolish things of the world to shame the wise and that he chose the weak things of the world to shame the strong. Why does God prefer to use those who are weak? "...so that no one may boast before him" (1 Cor. 1:29).

Do you want to be an "Elijah"? Do you want to go out in the power of the Holy Spirit and turn the tide in our idolatrous times? Do you want to be someone that God can use to "make ready a people prepared for the Lord?" If you feel weak, unworthy, and overwhelmed by the thought, then you qualify.

> Now [and then] Elijah the Tishbite, from Tishbe in Gilead, said to Ahab, "As the LORD, the God of Israel, lives, whom I serve, there will be neither dew nor rain in the next few years except at my word."

> (1 Kings 17:1)

What a statement! What boldness!! I have an idea. Why don't you call the President and tell him that he's been leading the country into sin, and that as the Lord lives, the stock market is going to crash and it's going to keep crashing until you say so. That's exactly what Elijah did in his day.

Why a drought? It was a direct challenge to those who followed Baal, the storm god. Notice that Elijah said, "As the Lord lives." He was saying, "The Lord is the living God. If your god Baal is a living god and if he really is the 'storm god' that controls the weather, then bring him on! Let him bring the rain. Let's see who brings rain on the earth." Elijah wanted to test the power of God over the power of their so-called god. Of course that was then, this is now, and we are way too sophisticated a people to believe in a storm god who controls the weather. I don't want to dwell here because I am from Minnesota, and in Minnesota, we already talk way too much about the weather. But the weather isn't really the point, is it? The point in this little corner of our story is - What is true? - Who is your God? If God is the Lord, then he must be your only God. You must trust him with all your needs and worship only him. In India, the Hindu people worship 330 million gods. I used to wonder how they could possibly have so many gods until I realized that they will worship just about anything. On one of my visits to India I was living in a small house about a quarter mile from the road. Every day when my driver came to pick me up, I walked the short path to meet him at the road. As I walked the same path several times a day, I noticed a rock about the size of a basketball sitting on a post about four feet off the ground. The rock served no visible purpose and each day as I passed it, I resisted the urge to knock it off the post. Finally, I asked my interpreter about the rock. He told me the rock was the "god" of that street. That gave me some insight into India's millions of gods. It may seem silly, but are we Americans really that much different? We will worship money, or a sports team, or a celebrity, or just about anything. To worship something is simply the thing you think about the most or rely on the most. The thing you are most passionate about is your god. Elijah's story tests us, just as it tested the Israelites long ago. Who or what will be your god? Where will you place your hope, faith, and trust?

What was the source of Elijah's confidence that made him so bold? Elijah was a man filled with the Spirit and he was also a man of God's Word. When God spoke, he listened.

Moses was another person who loved God's Word and in his farewell address to Israel, Moses encouraged the people to keep God's Word close:

Fix these words of mine in your hearts and minds; tie them as symbols on your hands and bind them on your foreheads. Teach them to your children, talking about them when you sit at home and when you walk along the road, when you lie down and when you get up. Write them on the doorframes of your houses and on your gates, so that your days and the days of your children may be many in the land that the LORD swore to give your forefathers, as many as the days that the heavens are above the earth.

(Deut. 11:18-21)

If you want to be an Elijah, you will have to fall in love with God's word, the Bible.

My hope for you as you read this book is that when you are done you will not be satisfied, but hungry, hungry to hear the infinite God of the Universe speak to you as a lover speaks to his bride. I pray that you will finish, panting for more.

In order for us to be people who can receive and pass-on God's love and power, the connection between us and God has to be two way. Elijah was not only a man of God's Word but also a man of prayer. More than a thousand years after Elijah lived the Bible still points out that he was a man of prayer:

> The prayer of a righteous man is powerful and effective. Elijah was a man just like us. He prayed earnestly that it would not rain, and it did not rain on the land for three and a half years. Again he prayed, and the heavens gave rain, and the earth produced its crops.
>
> (James 5:16-18)

Elijah was bold because he was backed by Jehovah himself. He wasn't acting on his own behalf but was merely acting as God's emissary. How did Elijah know that God would come through for him? He knew because he didn't stop the rain by his own power but was merely acting for God. He was a man of the Word and a man of prayer; both key for us if we want to operate in the power of the Holy Spirit.

Elijah was bold and strong. If his boldness and strength lie in himself, then he was a man to be envied and our story ends. But Elijah's strength didn't lie in himself. As we explore Elijah's story, we'll find that when his faith failed and he was cut off from his source of strength, he was a coward. And yet, when connected to his source, Elijah was a giant of a man without fear. Elijah himself gives us indication as to the source of his strength and courage: "As the LORD, the God of Israel lives." To the masses, Jehovah was a dead god. To Elijah, he lived. Does your God live? Elijah declared – "whom I serve," which literally means "before whom I stand." Elijah's God wasn't just alive but present. Is your God present? Is he with you every minute of the day? What does walking with God mean to you? Does your God live at the church building and do you just go visit him on Sundays? I wonder, what does God do all week long in that empty church building by himself? Don't laugh! Think about it. Does your God just show up at the beginning of each meal so you can thank him for it? Where is he the rest of the time? What does it really mean to walk with God?

The word, "Elijah" can mean either "Jehovah is my God" or "Jehovah is my strength." Elijah was merely living up to his name. Your name is Christian! You say, "But I'm only one person. How much can one person do?" One person can't do much on his own, but the Bible tells us, "we can do everything through him who gives us strength" (Phil. 4:13).

Life Lesson

_____

It doesn't matter how bad things get; God is never at a loss.

Consider and discuss: Think of a time when things seemed hopeless and at the last minute the circumstance just melted away? Do you think God came to your rescue just as things were at their worst?

God is the God of new beginnings. How has he helped you "start over" when you failed?

Do you have a sense that God "backs you up"? Are you able to be bold for Jesus because you know he is with you, or is this an area where God needs to help you grow?

The thing that you are the most passionate about is your god. Think about what you are passionate about, maybe a football or baseball team, or a music group? Name some of the gods that share your devotion to Jesus. Be honest.

Is your God present? Is he with you every minute of the day? What does "walking with God" mean to you? List a pivotal time in your life and record how you saw God's presence during that time. How does that assist you with trusting God in your current circumstance?

CHAPTER 4

He Kerith for You

Then the word of the Lord came to Elijah: "Leave here, turn eastward and hide in the Kerith Ravine, east of the Jordan. You will drink from the brook, and I have ordered the ravens to feed you there." So he did what the Lord had told him. He went to the Kerith Ravine, east of the Jordan, and stayed there. The ravens brought him bread and meat in the morning and bread and meat in the evening, and he drank from the brook.

(1Kings 17:2-6)

We have established that Elijah was a man of the Word and also a man of prayer, prerequisites for what came next. "Then the word of the Lord came to Elijah." Our prophet was bold enough to confront King Ahab because he was close to Jehovah; now we see that same closeness is the source of his new direction.

We should seek to hear God's voice, to know his marching orders when they come. I'm not suggesting that we audibly hear God's voice although he may speak to us that way. I think that most of the time we will hear God's voice in a more subtle way, through the voice of a loved one, or through current circumstances. Often God's voice is a quiet nudging. We must be listening, always paying attention. God does speak to us and if we are expecting it, we will hear his voice. We can test that "quiet nudging" by how it agrees with God's written word. God will never contradict what he has told us in the Bible. One word of caution, God will very often give us marching orders that to our finite minds make no sense. He does this both to test us and also because he has an eternal perspective that we lack. When seeking God's voice you cannot use your human reasoning to judge the reasonableness of God's direction for your life. We must learn to walk by faith rather than by sight.

God told Elijah to hide in the Kerith Ravine. Why hide? Our bold prophet would go on to do some pretty amazing things for God. His destiny was Mount Carmel where he would defeat all the prophets of the false gods. Sure, Ahab was a powerful king; but with God, Elijah was invincible. Why would God send him into hiding? Why retreat? Victory is calling! In my book, "Moses - Steps to a Life of Faith," I asked the same question about Moses. God's plan for Moses was that he would lead the entire nation of Israel out of Egypt and into the Promised Land. Why then did he need to spend 40 years living on the backside of the desert? Why the Kerith Ravine for Elijah? Could it be that both Moses and Elijah were not ready for the dream God had for them but had to go through a period of preparation first? God does the same with us. He often brings circumstances into our lives that we process as failure but he sees them as preparation. God sent Elijah to Kerith because he wasn't ready for Mount Carmel.

We often think that after some time of working or ministering we need to rest, but here God sent Elijah to Kerith before his great adventure on Mount Carmel. Can you see any advantage in that? I wonder if Elijah was a little full of himself after his bold encounter with Ahab. I wonder if Elijah was tempted to think he was a big shot now. I wonder if Elijah was too strong for God to use at Carmel and so he sent him to Kerith. Can we be too strong for God to use us? Not only is it possible, but I think it is often the case. I don't know about you, but when God reveals a part of his dream for me my first inclination is to get excited and go after it. I often find myself out in front of God and relying on my own strength. God knows that I will fail without him and he loves me too much to see me crash and burn; and so, he sends me to Kerith.

It's a solid principle. Remember Gideon? He had thirty thousand men to fight the Midianites; he and his army were vastly out-numbered, but God was with them.

Since God was going to give Gideon a great victory over his enemy, and God wanted Gideon to know that the victory was really God's, not his, God had Gideon send home all those who were afraid. Twenty thousand went home. Then God had Gideon test the ten thousand that remained by having them drink water. He sent home those who kneeled down to drink but he kept those who lapped the water by bringing it to their mouths. After this test, Gideon had only three hundred men left to fight many thousands of Midianites, just the kind of odds God loves to work with. You probably know the story. God gave Gideon and Israel a great victory that day.

In another example, Jesus' disciples had been out ministering in his name. They had healed the sick and cast out demons. Many had come to believe that the Messiah had truly come. When they came back to Jesus, they began to excitedly tell him about the miracles they had performed. Jesus responded, "...Come with me by yourselves to a quiet place and get some rest. So they went away by themselves in a boat to a solitary place" (Mark 6:31-32). Because we are too independent from God and too confident in our own strength, God will bring us to our Keriths to be quieted and sustained by him. Often, we feel like we are doing something wrong when we retreat from things, and yet sometimes it's part of God's plan for us to just quit being busy and fall back on him. "He makes me lie down in green pastures; he leads me beside quiet waters" (Ps. 23:2).

A spiritual disease plagues many today, especially Christians. Many of us have been taught first by our parents and then the church, that a good work ethic is part of being a good Christian. There is an old, old saying that "idleness is the devil's workshop." You don't hear that saying much today, but the disease is still with us. We all need to learn to listen only to the voice of the Spirit. When the Spirit tells us to get busy, we should jump, and when the Spirit tells us to stay put we should obey. Actually, the devil wants you to be busy all the time. He wants you so busy that in doing "things" you never have time to sit on Jesus' lap so he can just caress your face. "The LORD your God is with you, he is mighty to save. He will take great delight in you, he will quiet you with his love, he will rejoice over you with singing" (Zeph. 3:17).

Think about the following questions:

How would you react if you lost your job this week?

How would you respond to God if all of a sudden you were laid up with a serious illness?

How do you respond when one day you realize that the dreams you had as a young person will never be realized?

How will you manage when you are let down by the one you love?

The word, "Kerith" literally means "the place of failure." It's an old, dried-up river bed. It's a place of death where nothing is happening. God uses our failures to bring us back into dependence on him, the place where he can care for us and love us up and wipe the tears from our cheeks. God hid Elijah at the brook Kerith. At what Kerith is he quieting you? - the Kerith of sickness, the Kerith of dashed dreams, or the Kerith of a broken heart? To what place of solitude will he send you to bring you low before God so that he can raise you up before others?

> Show the wonder of your great love, you who save by your right hand those who take refuge in you from their foes. Keep me as the apple of your eye; hide me in the shadow of your wings.

> (Ps. 17:7-8)

We've considered how God was able to use Elijah as a channel of his power. I wonder if that channel, which is so evidently displayed at Carmel, is formed and opened at Kerith. I wonder if before we can be raised up on our Mount Carmel, we have to be brought low at our brook Kerith. I am a little suspect of Christian leaders whose rise to fame isn't interrupted by some failures. Failure is how God schools us.

Another reason that God sent Elijah to Kerith may have been to teach him to trust. "You will drink from the brook, and I have ordered the ravens to feed you there." There is strong emphasis on the word *there*. Kerith was the place that God sent Elijah so he could be dependent on God and God could meet his needs. There may have been better places for Elijah to go, but Kerith was the place where God had sent him and Kerith was the place where God was obligated to meet his needs. If we are in the place where God wants us to be he will always take care of us by whatever miracles necessary.

If we follow God's lead, he will always take care of us. The manna always accompanies the pillar of cloud.

> So do not worry, saying, 'What shall we eat?' or 'What shall we drink?' or 'What shall we wear?' For the pagans run after all these things, and your heavenly Father knows that you need them. But seek first his kingdom and his righteousness, and all these things will be given to you as well.

(Matt. 6:31-33)

Imagine Elijah's first morning at the brook as he arose from sleeping on his bed of soft moss and took a drink at the bubbling brook. The ravens landed on his nose and shoved that delicious road pizza into his mouth. This is the life, he thought. How good it is to be cared for by God and to rest in his wonderful provision. Elijah spends most of his days praying. If he had a Bible he would have read verses like Phil 4:19: "And my God will meet all your needs according to his glorious riches in Christ Jesus."

> "Sometime later the brook dried up because there had been no rain in the land."

> (1 Kings 17:7)

Now picture Elijah a year later. He hasn't heard from the Lord. The moss has dried up and blown away. He sleeps on bare rock now. The brook has dried up and there is nothing left to drink from but a muddy pool. He drinks by squeezing mud through a sock. The road pizza was good but it's getting a little old now. Where is Jehovah, he thinks? Did he forget me here? If I were Elijah I'd be making plans. The problem solver in me would kick in and I'd be coming up with all the alternatives. Where can I go? Where will I find water? I have to get out of here. This place of life has become a place of death. What would you do? The question is: Are we willing to wait on God when we're at our Kerith or are we going to take matters into our own hands? God had placed Elijah at Kerith with instructions to stay there. Are we willing to stay in the place where God has sent us even though it doesn't make sense? Are we willing to stay until we hear his next instruction?

King Saul is an example of a man who was not willing to wait. Saul was in a tough spot. The Philistines had come to fight against Israel with a very large army. The Israelites were afraid, their army had scattered, and they were in hiding. Saul desperately needed a word from the Lord, so he did the right thing, he sent for Samuel the priest. Samuel was to come in seven days and offer a sacrifice to the Lord. Saul dutifully waited the appointed seven days but Samuel didn't come. The army was scattering and Saul was desperate for a word from God. "Where is Samuel?!" Finally Saul decided to take matters into his own hands and so he sacrificed the burnt offering himself. It sounds to me that Saul didn't really do anything too wrong. Sure, only a priest was to offer the sacrifice, but

Samuel was late and the Philistines were on their way. What's a king to do? When Samuel finally arrived he had some harsh words for King Saul:

> "You acted foolishly," Samuel said. "You have not kept the command the LORD your God gave you; if you had, he would have established your kingdom over Israel for all time. But now your kingdom will not endure; the LORD has sought out a man after his own heart and appointed him leader of his people, because you have not kept the LORD's command."

> (1 Sam. 13:13-14)

If only Saul had waited just a few hours more. "I wait for the Lord, my soul waits, and in his word I put my hope" (Ps. 130:5).

The lesson of the dried-up brook:

Have you spent time alongside drying brooks? Maybe you are sitting beside a drying brook today, a drying brook of health, or a drying brook of finances. Maybe your job is an old dried up brook with no future or maybe you are stuck at a drying brook of strained friendships or a broken relationship. It's hard to sit beside a drying brook. Kerith is the place of failure. It's hard to just sit there and wait for the next step to be revealed, much harder even than facing the prophets of Baal on Mount Carmel. "Be still, and know that I am God; I will be exalted among the nations, I will be exalted in the earth" (Ps. 46:10).

God led Elijah to the brook. He gave him the bubbling water, soft moss, and ravens as gifts. Why would he now let the brook dry up? Why does God let brooks dry up? Why does he allow his children to fail? When our brooks dry up, it seems like a bad thing to us; but God allows failure to get our attention so we will listen for his voice taking us on to the next step in our great adventure. He wants to teach us the lessons of relying on him to meet our needs. Are we listening? God wants us to learn to trust in him, not his gifts. It's the lesson of the dried-up brook. God let the brook dry up so that Elijah would turn from it to him. He will do no less for us!

He will take the cheap water away so that we can enjoy the water of life...his Spirit.

> Jesus answered, "Everyone who drinks this water will be thirsty again, but whoever drinks the water I give him will never thirst. Indeed, the water I give him will become in him a spring of water welling up to eternal life."

> (John 4:13-14)

Unbelief looks at God through circumstances (dried up brooks) and asks ...why? Faith looks at circumstances through God's eyes... and praises him!

Life Lesson

Responding to Failure

Consider and discuss: Is it possible for a person to be too strong for God to use? When you fail, are you likely to blame God or yourself. Have you considered that God may have a part in your failure? Do you think that God will sometimes let you fail because he has a blessing for you that you are not yet prepared to receive? Could it be that God has an adventure for you, but you must first be prepared?

Think of a time in your life where God dealt with you in this way. List some times in your past that you would characterize as "failure." Can you see the hand of God in those times now that you look back on them?

When failure comes, are you prone to take matters into our own hands or do you embrace it and learn from the experience?

At what current "Kerith" is God quieting you? What major obstacle in your life might actually be God drawing you to his lap?

CHAPTER 5

Into the Smelting Furnace

Only after the brook was dry and the ravens gone did Jehovah speak:

> Then the word of the LORD came to him: "Go at once to Zarephath of Sidon and stay there. I have commanded a widow in that place to supply you with food."

> (1 Kings 17:8-9)

And so, the Lord moves Elijah to his next adventure and his next place of growth. And that is what the Lord does with us. God wants to build Christ-like character into our lives; he does it by leading us from adventure to adventure, with each stop along the way a lesson to be learned. Someone said, "Life is just one darned thing after another." It's not true. Our circumstances are not random, but designed by God to lead us into what is best for us. Why? Because he loves us! Someone else said, "Success is merely going enthusiastically from failure to failure."

So why does God lead us by allowing us to fail? There is a prosperity gospel theology that teaches that if you have enough faith, God will only bring good things, including riches and happiness, into your life. The truth lies in an obscure verse in the Old Testament book of Jeremiah:

> Moab has been at rest from youth, like wine left on its dregs, not poured from one jar to another-- she has not gone into exile. So she tastes as she did, and her aroma is unchanged.
>
> (Jer. 48:11)

Jeremiah was prophesying against the land of Moab, saying that since that nation had not gone into exile, she had not grown. In order to understand this verse you have to understand how wine was made. Originally, fermented grape juice is thick, impure, and smelly. It was left in kegs until the thick sediment precipitated to the bottom. Then the clearer liquid was carefully poured off. This process was repeated over and over until the wine was clear, pure, sweet and with a light aroma. This is how God purifies us. He pours us from circumstance to circumstance, each time leaving some of the dregs behind. Some of this pouring out is a painful process for us, and yet from each "pouring out" experience, we come out purer and sweeter.

Understand the process. If the wine was not left to sit quietly it would not be purified. As God pours us from circumstance to circumstance, if we do not submit to the process, we are left bitter. But if we allow God the freedom to have his way, trust him to bring both the rain and the sun, the failures and successes will all work together to make us more like his son.

> And we know that in all things God works for the good of those who love him, who have been called according to his purpose. For those God foreknew he also

> predestined to be conformed to the likeness of his Son, that he might be the firstborn among many brothers.
>
> (Rom. 8:28-29)

Elijah had been poured from Ahab to Kerith, and was now about to be poured to Zarephath. God was moving him from circumstance to circumstance in his life, failure to failure, and from hardship to hardship, all to prepare him for victory on Mount Carmel.

Now, if I was Elijah, I might have been tempted to argue a bit with God about this next assignment. If I had spent untold days and nights sitting beside that brook going over all the possible courses of action, going to Zarephath wouldn't be one of them. Zarephath was one-hundred miles away, through Ahab territory, and into the homeland of Queen Jezebel. The Sidonian gods of Phoenicia would have home-field advantage. Elijah would be on their turf. It was often believed that the gods were territorial. Apparently, even Abraham believed this; he feared that God could not protect him outside the Promised Land (see

Gen. 20:11-13). This was also true of the Syrians, who thought that Yahweh was the "god of the mountain," while Baal was "god of the valley" (1 Kings 20:28). If this was true, then Elijah would be taking a huge risk by going to Zarephath, the home base of Jezebel's gods.

Of course, we know that the one true God is God everywhere. Zarephath was actually the safest place in the world for Elijah. Why? Because that was the place that God had sent him. The safest place in the world for us is where God tells us to be.

If you are where God has sent you, you are invincible.

Zarephath was in the very heart of Baalism, enemy turf. And there Elijah was supposed to be cared for by a heathen widow woman; not a very classy assignment for an important man of God. He wouldn't have minded so much to help her, but to be dependent on her, well that was humbling.

Since God sent Elijah to Zarephath to be cared for by a widow, we should spend some time looking at widows. Being a widow in those days was much different than today. It's important for us to be aware of the status of women in the ancient secular world. Women had no rights or value in themselves. A woman only had worth because she was associated with a man. The man could be her father or later her husband; but without a father or a husband, a woman was a non-entity. Women weren't allowed to own land or transact business. And so my wife, Barb, would only have worth as a person because she is of the house of Saffrin! She would have no worth as a person aside from being associated with her husband. Are you women glad you live now, rather than then? Women were not allowed to work or go out in public without their husbands. Women not wearing proper attire in public were beaten or stoned. Homes where women were present would have the windows covered so she couldn't be seen by outsiders. Women were required to wear silent shoes so they would not disturb any man. Women were considered sub-human and could be stoned to death, even if they were with their husbands, if they showed as much as one square inch of skin in public or if they offend a man in any way.

How would you like to have been a woman in those days? Actually, this is the plight of many women in extremist Muslim countries today. A human rights report I read some time ago said that a woman had been stoned to death after her sleeve blew up because she had her arm on the open window of the car she was in as a passenger.

In Old Testament times, among the pagans, there was one class of people that were even lower on the social scale than women...widows. A widow was the dregs of society. Today we have compassion for widows, hold them in high esteem, and society goes to great lengths to help them. In the ancient pagan world they had no value and were just left to fend for themselves or die.

With this background on the social status of widows of the day, you can imagine how Elijah felt when he heard Jehovah say that he was to go to Zarephath where a widow would be taking care of him. Elijah was a man just like us, and yet God was able to use him in mighty ways. That's why we want to study Elijah's life. Elijah had his Mount Carmel where he defeated God's enemies and turned the people of Israel back to the worship of the one true God. We study Elijah because God has a Mount Carmel for each of us. There is no limit to what God can accomplish through one single sold-out life. God wants us to be a channel of his power to turn the tide in the pagan world we live in. But as we've seen so far, Elijah wasn't ready to go meet the enemies of God. God needed to bring him through some experiences first to get him ready. We've seen how Jehovah sent him to the brook Kerith were he could rest and be sustained by God's supply of food and water, a place where he was alone with God. Kerith means "failure," and we've seen how God often uses failure in our lives to get us to lean on him and re-establish our dependence on him. Now that Elijah had learned to depend on Jehovah to meet his needs it was time to be on to the next adventure. Jehovah says, "I've taught you how to rest in me at Kerith and now I'm going to refine the pride out of you at Zarephath." Zarephath means "smelting-furnace." After the smelting-furnace, Elijah would be ready for Mount Carmel.

> Then the word of the LORD came to him: "Go at once to Zarephath of Sidon and stay there. I have commanded a widow in that place to supply you with food."

> (1 Kings 17:8-9)

Let's take a quick look at King Ahab and see how he fits into the story. Ahab was Elijah's adversary. His people looked up to him and trusted him to provide their help and spiritual guidance in this desperate time. He was the king. He was living in the castle. He was popular, and he was living in relative luxury. He was "the man!" How was Elijah going to compete with the mighty King Ahab for the hearts of the people while living with an insignificant widow woman, considered by her own people to be the dregs of the earth? She was just a despised widow with a starving son. How will God's plan possibly help Elijah gain credibility, respect, and honor among the people so they will accept him as their spiritual leader?

This doesn't seem like a very good idea and yet it is the clear will of God for Elijah. This is what it means to be obedient. It means to obey the will of the father even when it doesn't make earthly sense. It means to trust in him and realize that he loves us and knows what is best for us. To be willfully disobedient is to say to God that we know better than he does or that we question his love. God had made Elijah's direction clear. He said go to Zarephath and stay there. "I have commanded a widow in that place."

God's path of blessing was clear for Elijah, yet it made no earthly sense. Are you in the place of blessing? Are you where God wants you today? You know being a person of faith doesn't mean that you never question God, but neither does it mean that you only follow him when it makes sense.

True faith is born in following God into the smelting-furnace...following him into a scary, humbling place that makes no earthly sense, but following because you trust him.

> Go at once to Zarephath of Sidon and stay there. I have commanded a widow in that place to supply you with food. So he went to Zarephath. When he came to the town gate, a widow was there gathering sticks. He called to her and asked, "Would you bring me a little water in a jar so I may have a drink?" As she was going to get it, he called, "And bring me, please, a piece of bread".

> (1 Kings 17:9-11)

"So he went." Faith is obeying God even when it doesn't make sense. Courage is when you go in spite of your fear.

Elijah arrived at Zarephath after hiking 100 miles through mostly barren land, avoiding settlements because he was a wanted man. I imagine that as he arrived at Zarephath, he was exhausted, thirsty and hungry. He was probably apprehensive about meeting this woman who was supposed to take care of him. Most likely God didn't reveal much about what he is going to do ahead of time. Elijah's virtue wasn't that he had no doubts; but rather that he obeyed God in spite of his doubts. Imagine Elijah approaching the city gates. He couldn't wait to meet the widow who was to give him water and food and lodging. Imagine how he felt when he saw this emaciated woman, nothing but skin and bones, barely able to walk, literally starving to death. This can't be right, he thought. This can't be the person that Jehovah meant to help me. He looked around and saw the town in a terrible state. The drought had ravaged this place worse than most. This wasn't the place for Elijah. This can't be right, he thought. What am I doing here?

What would you do in this circumstance? If you are like me, you often try to run away from your problems, blame others, or God. Sometimes in the midst of a crisis, we plug our ears to God's corrective voice, or just crumble in despair. We pray, "God, get me out of here!" I can imagine Elijah praying, "Lord, this isn't the place for me!" I picture God answering, "Elijah, it's not just about you." The picture is always bigger than just us. The world doesn't revolve around us. God always has a global, big-picture plan. The good news is that there are no losers in God's economy. It's always win-win. But in order to win, you have to follow him really close because his plan is larger than you can know or see.

To be in the place of blessing you have to stay close to the master planner.

If only we knew that God has designed the Zarephaths in our lives to prepare us for the Mount Carmels, we would pray, "Lord, teach me your ways," instead of, "Lord, get me out of here." Instead of giving up or falling back on self-reliance, we would submit to our circumstances and declare, "The Lord He is God. Blessed be the name of the Lord."

> Anyone who intends to come with me has to let me lead. You're not in the driver's seat; I am. Don't run from suffering; embrace it. Follow me and I'll show you how.
>
> (Matt. 16:24 Message Bible)

If you're going to dance with God, you have to let him lead.

What's different about Zarephath as compared to Kerith? Both were places for Elijah to go to learn to be dependent on God. What was different? Zarephath had people. God may have big projects for us to accomplish but you can bet that his focus is always going to be people. Don't forget the widow woman, her son, and their importance in God's eyes. He sent his son to die for the likes of them. This lowly woman lives on the same street in heaven that Elijah does.

Why this widow? She wasn't even an Israelite?

> "I tell you the truth," he continued, "no prophet is accepted in his hometown. I assure you that there were many widows in Israel in Elijah's time, when the sky was shut for three and a half years and there was a severe famine throughout the land. Yet Elijah was not sent to any of them, but to a widow in Zarephath in the region of Sidon."

> (Luke 4:24-26)

God sent Elijah to someone who would accept him. God may bring you into unlikely circumstances in your life in order to bless you with someone who will accept you the way you are. He may even take you to Zarephath, the smelting-furnace, in order to bless you through an unlikely person. Our lesson in all of this is that we must come to the place where we stop second guessing God and just submit to his leading. We may not understand what he is doing, but we just follow him.

Why would God choose this woman? She had been living in her own hell. Her son was probably at home, too weak to come and help her gather a couple of sticks to build a fire to prepare their last meal and then die. If the Lord needed someone to take care of Elijah, why would he pick this woman? Why not pick someone with resources? Before God could use Elijah to stand for truth on Mount Carmel, he had to first refine the pride out of his life. "Anything...that can withstand fire must be put through the fire, and then it will be clean" (Num. 31:23). The Lord puts us through the fire. He immerses us in the smelting-furnace, not to destroy us, but to purify us.

We are put into the fire by hands of love, meant not to consume us but to consume that which binds us.

Circumstances were depressing for both Elijah and the widow. God put them together to bless them both. Their difficulties became to their faith as weights to a weight-lifter. God used the two of them to strengthen and support each other. Elijah needed the woman's faith added to his so that Jehovah could bless them both. Jehovah selected her for her faith, not her gender, her political status, her religious affiliation or her resources. Her mustard-seed faith released the resources of God Almighty. What is the lesson for us in this? Again, if you're going to dance with God you have to let him lead.

Life Lesson

The smelting pot - Learning the process that God will use to purify and refine us.

Consider and discuss: What victory is God preparing for you? Ask yourself today about the "stuff" in your life. The world is wrong. "Stuff" doesn't just happen. God loves you too much to just let life be random. He uses every little circumstance to draw you to himself and to clean out of you everything that wasn't his idea. Are you submitting to his leading today? Are you submitting to his authority and his sovereignty? Think about what faith you have exercised lately that has released the resources of God.

Can you think of a time when you had to humble yourself before God could work? Do you run away from difficult situations or embrace them as having come from the Lord? How does the statement, "If you are going to dance with God, you have to let him lead," make you feel?

Think of a time when you knew God's will in a circumstance, but it just made no sense, a time you were sure you knew a better way. How did you handle it? In what area of your life do you find obedience the most difficult? Has God led you anywhere that you never thought you'd go?

CHAPTER 6

The Unknown Road

My guess is that Jehovah didn't reveal his plan to Elijah much in advance, but that he just continually gave him the next step. The call to go to Zarephath probably wasn't followed by detailed instructions about what to do or what would happen next. God's desire for us to walk in faith often results in us taking an unknown road. Often we are afraid of what we don't know. God understands our fears, but faith requires that we face the unknown road in spite of our fears. I wonder how many great adventures I've missed because I was afraid to take that first step when God said, "Go."

Elijah wasn't the only person in the Bible asked to trust God on an unknown road. Once upon a time, God went to the most sophisticated city on earth to find a man and a woman that would give up everything and follow him on an unknown road for a promise...and he found them.

> The Lord had said to Abram, "Leave your country, your people and your father's household and go to the land I will show you."
>
> (Gen. 12:1)

Think about this. Abram and his wife Sarai were being asked by Jehovah God to leave their sophisticated lifestyle and their beautiful city with all of the accoutrements of modern living. They were being asked to leave their family and friends behind, to leave everything they have spent their lives building, and leave it for some anonymous dot on a distant map. How could they even possibly consider this?

Look, when you are young you may leave everything behind and not even look back as you anticipate a new adventure and a new life. When I was in my 20's, my company transferred me to Tucson, Arizona. Barb and I strapped the playpen to the roof of the car and off we went, no looking back, no questioning. It was high adventure. But things change as you get older, don't they? If you are over fifty you know what I'm talking about. It's harder to hang on to that adventurous spirit as you get older. In our story, Abram is seventy-five years old. I can hear him argue, "What are you talking about Lord? - Go where? - Do what? Lord don't you know that I'm retired!"

Consider Moses. Two-thirds of the way through his life, at the age of 80, God called Moses on the backside of the wilderness and he said, "Now I'm ready to use you."

I thought when I got to be 60, life would be slowing down. Good news for those who thought you had to be young to do great things for God. No, you can be young or old, but whatever your age, you have to be ready to saddle up when he calls.

God may call you at any age, but when he calls you, he will call you out of your comfort zone and onto an unknown, scary road. But along with the calling will come a promise. God told Abram that if he would leave his country, his own people, and the security of his father's house, that he would give Abram not only the heir that he yearned for but a whole nation of children. Abram heard these words and I imagine his jaw dropped. I can hear him say, "Come on God. You've got to be kidding me. I'm seventy-five years old and Sarai's no spring chicken either. We have no children and our time is past. It's too late for me!" Abram's dream had become impossible, but God had promised it, and he is the God of the impossible. Today, 4.5 billion of the world's seven billion people call Abram "father". The Jews, Christians, and Muslims all look to Abram as their father. God called Abram to leave all that was valuable to him and sent him to a place where God could fulfill his greatest dream. Sarai wanted a child; Abram wanted an heir. God gave them 4.5 billion.

Life Lessons

God's desire for us to walk in faith often results in us taking an unknown road. Often we are afraid of the unknown. God understands our fears but faith requires that we face the unknown road in spite of our fears.

Consider and discuss: Obeying God when it doesn't make sense, finding the place of blessing. Think about Abram being called out of that modern, sophisticated city, called to a wilderness and a life of hardship and scratching for every need. How would you respond? Would you see it as high adventure or foolish risk?

The unknown road has huge rewards, but are we willing to face the fears and learn to be a risk-taker with God? I wonder how many times we hear the voice of God, and because what we hear is so out of our comfort zone, we just write off the "voice" as last night's bad pizza.

Faith means we act in accordance with what we know, and we know he is faithful!

To what "unknown roads has God called you in the past? Is he calling you today?

Write a simple prayer asking God to either forgive you for not listening to his voice because you were afraid, or to empower you and give you courage to cooperate with his plan even if you don't know the next step. Ask him to show you the unknown road to blessing that he has prepared for you.

CHAPTER 7

When Tragedy Strikes

"As surely as the LORD your God lives," she replied, "I don't have any bread-- only a handful of flour in a jar and a little oil in a jug. I am gathering a few sticks to take home and make a meal for myself and my son that we may eat it-- and die." Elijah said to her, "Don't be afraid. Go home and do as you have said. But first make a small cake of bread for me from what you have and bring it to me, and then make something for yourself and your son. For this is what the LORD, the God of Israel, says: "The jar of flour will not be used up and the jug of oil will not run dry until the day the LORD gives rain on the land." She went away and did as Elijah had told her. So there was food every day for Elijah and for the woman and her family. For the jar of flour was not used up and the jug of oil did not run dry, in keeping with the word of the LORD spoken by Elijah.

(1 Kings 17:12-16)

When God puts you into the smelting-furnace to refine the pride out of you, he will supply all your needs if you will submit to the process and trust him. The woman was desperate. God called her out of her own despair, her own dried-up brook. He called her in the midst of her circumstance to bless her if she would trust him. Sometimes when you are down to the end of yourself, sometimes when you are on the side of a cliff hanging on by a thread, Jehovah will ask you to let go. It's a test of your faith. Sometimes you have to let go and believe God.

One day when Jesus was visiting the temple and he saw one poor widow putting her two worthless coins into the offering he recognized that she was giving all that she had to God. Jesus pointed out to his disciples that in God's

> eyes, she had given more than anyone else: "I tell you the truth, this poor widow has put more into the treasury than all the others. They all gave out of their wealth; but she, out of her poverty, put in everything — all she had to live on."

(Mark 12:43-44)

Often we are reluctant to give of ourselves because we're stretched. Maybe we judge what we do as insignificant. Elijah's widow friend only had one small bit of flour to feed him, not enough to sustain him for long. In another story, the widow at the temple gave two cents. It hardly made a difference in the temple budget. And yet it was the faith and willingness of these two women to give what they had that pleased God.

God only requires all of us, all of who we are and all that we have.

He wants us to be at his disposal. You don't have to be gifted or have resources for God's love and power to flow through you; you just have to be available. If you have a desire to be used of God, he will empower and enrich you. Elijah's new-found widow friend didn't have to struggle to perform.

She just responded with the faith and the flour she had.

> Sometime later the son of the woman who owned the house became ill. He grew worse and worse, and finally stopped breathing
>
> (1 Kings 17:17)

What's this all about? How does this tragic event tie into our story? Elijah and this woman are linked together as unlikely partners in this saga. We know that God is in control. Nothing happens that doesn't traverse the cross first. There are no accidents or unlucky events. God is on the throne of the universe. So what is Jehovah up to now with the death of the woman's son? What is God's purpose in this?

> She said to Elijah, "What do you have against me, man of God? Did you come to remind me of my sin and kill my son?"
>
> (1 Kings 17:18)

I find it interesting that the woman's first response to this situation is guilt. She said literally, "Why have you drawn God's attention to me, man of God?" The woman assumed that Elijah's presence had drawn

God's attention to her and her sins. Her perception of God was that when her sins were discovered, she would be punished, and that was why her son was dead. She pictured God looking down waiting for her to sin so he could pounce. How would you rate the accuracy of her perception? Is that the God you know? I think if we were to take a poll of believers we would find that the majority of practicing Christians would say that the woman's perception of God was wrong. I think most would say that God is a compassionate God; yet I have witnessed many Christians respond just like this woman when they experience a crisis. On the cross Jesus cried out, "Father, forgive them, for they do not know what they are doing." Those words reflect the heart of God. The woman needed a new picture of Elijah's God. Often we miss the place of blessing because we have a false picture of God. God was about to give this woman a new revelation of himself.

Life Lessons

God only requires all of us, all of who we are and all that we have.

Consider and discuss: When you are in the smelting-furnace, if you submit to God's process, he will take care of your needs. Can you think of a time in your life when this was true for you? Maybe it was a time when you were struggling financially and that unexpected check came in the mail. Or maybe it was a time when you were feeling down and that phone call of encouragement lifted you.

Think of a time when difficulties or crisis struck you or your family. Looking back can you see God's purpose in it? What was your first response? Did you assume that God was punishing you because of your sin?

CHAPTER 8

Graduation Day

God had a purpose in this crisis. Elijah had been in school at Kerith and Zarephath. God taught him how to be dependent at Kerith, and how to be humble at Zarephath. The death of the woman's son was Elijah's graduation day, his final exam. As Moses stood before a burning bush at his graduation, so Elijah stood before the widow's dead son. It's time for Jehovah to test Elijah. God brings four tests for Elijah to test his readiness for Mount Carmel. It's time for Elijah to flex his spiritual muscles. The woman said to Elijah, "What do you have against me, man of God? Did you come to remind me of my sin and kill my son?" How would Elijah react to this strong statement?

> "Give me your son," Elijah replied. He took him from her arms, carried him to the upper room where he was staying, and laid him on his bed.
>
> (1 Kings 17:19)

Elijah gently took the boy in his arms and carried him to the upper room. Elijah had learned the gentleness of God at Kerith and Zarephath, and he displays it here. How we react when we are challenged and accused is a measure of the degree that we have given up our rights and sold out to the work of the gentle Spirit of God in our lives.

Elijah had passed the test of gentleness.

Then he cried out to the LORD:

> O LORD my God, have you brought tragedy also upon this widow I am staying with, by causing her son to die?
>
> (1 Kings 17:20)

He cried out to the Lord. The word "cry" here is a thunderous scream, a yell, a desperate bleating. Elijah was quick to realize that he was powerless in himself and that all his hope rested in God.

Elijah had passed the test of dependence on God.

> Then he stretched himself out on the boy three times and cried to the LORD, "O LORD my God, let this boy's life return to him!"
>
> (1 Kings 17:21)

For an Israelite, to touch a dead body made him unclean; he would feel he had defiled himself. Elijah had to give up on any thoughts he had of being a big shot. He had to get dirty to save the boy. Some will never know the Savior unless we stoop to where they are to give them a hand-up.

Elijah had passed the test of humility.

He stretched himself out on the boy three times.

Elijah didn't give up. He wasn't easily discouraged.

Elijah had passed the test of perseverance.

> The LORD heard Elijah's cry, and the boy's life returned to him, and he lived. Elijah picked up the child and carried him down from the room into the house. He gave him to his mother and said, "Look, your son is alive!" Then the woman said to Elijah, "Now I know that you are a man of God and that the word of the LORD from your mouth is the truth."
>
> (1 Kings 17:22-24)

The woman's faith was rewarded and Elijah's faith was strengthened. Elijah had been sent to Zarephath to be humbled, to bring faith and hope to a desperate woman and to demonstrate the power of God that would bring him to Mount Carmel. The woman was there to be given a whole new picture of God, to be strengthened in faith and to receive the blessing of God on her life and her family. Two unlikely people brought together in unlikely circumstances to receive a blessing from each other and Jehovah, and to be the spark that re-ignited the Israelites to the worship of the one true God. Elijah would never be the same. The woman would never be the same.

Elijah had passed the tests. He was ready for victory at Carmel.

Life Lessons

God has a purpose in crisis. Often a crisis is the final exam before a great victory.

Consider and discuss: Think of a crisis time in your life that you could call your "graduation day." Was the Lord using this time to test you just prior to a great adventure?

Think about lessons the Lord has taught you through failures and a time when you were able to use those lessons to help someone else.

How does God want you to respond to Him after what he's shown you in this chapter?

CHAPTER 9

Obadiah

This chapter gives us a contrast between a weak man who feared God and a strong man who feared people.

We are studying Elijah because we see all the power that flowed through him, and we yearn to be strong and mighty like he was, bold and fearless in the face of the struggles we encounter. Life quickly teaches us that spiritual power is not one of those things you can, "fake it until you make it." We do not generate spiritual power on our own; rather the Holy Spirit's power flows through us. In fact, our quest is not to "be powerful" but merely to have God's power flow through us. Elijah became a coward when his connection to God was weakened. Some people only want to be known as people with the power of God. They care more about what other people think of them than they care about what God thinks of them. As we read the next little piece of Elijah's story, a new character is introduced. Obadiah gives us a contrast between a good person trying to live in his own strength and Elijah who has tapped into the power of the living God.

> After a long time, in the third year, the word of the LORD came to Elijah: "Go and present yourself to Ahab, and I will send rain on the land." So Elijah went to present himself to Ahab. Now the famine was severe in Samaria, and Ahab had summoned Obadiah, who was in charge of his palace. (Obadiah was a devout believer in the LORD. While Jezebel was killing off the LORD's prophets, Obadiah had taken a hundred prophets and hidden them in two caves, fifty in each, and had supplied them with food and water.) Ahab had said to Obadiah, "Go through the land to all the springs and valleys. Maybe we can find some grass to

keep the horses and mules alive so we will not have to kill any of our animals." So they divided the land they were to cover, Ahab going in one direction and Obadiah in another. As Obadiah was walking along, Elijah met him. Obadiah recognized him, bowed down to the ground, and said, "Is it really you, my lord Elijah?" "Yes," he replied. "Go tell your master, 'Elijah is here.'" "What have I done wrong," asked Obadiah, "that you are handing your servant over to Ahab to be put to death? As surely as the LORD your God lives, there is not a nation or kingdom where my master has not sent someone to look for you. And whenever a nation or kingdom claimed you were not there, he made them swear they could not find you. But now you tell me to go to my master and say, 'Elijah is here.' I don't know where the Spirit of the LORD may carry you when I leave you. If I go and tell Ahab and he doesn't find you, he will kill me. Yet I your servant have worshiped the LORD since my youth. Haven't you heard, my lord, what I did while Jezebel was killing the prophets of the LORD? I hid a hundred of the LORD's prophets in two caves, fifty in each, and supplied them with food and water. And now you tell me to go to my master and say, 'Elijah is here.' He will kill me!" Elijah said, "As the LORD Almighty lives, whom I serve, I will surely present myself to Ahab today." So, Obadiah went to meet Ahab and told him, and Ahab went to meet Elijah.

(1 Kings 18:1-16)

What do you think of Obadiah? He was an official in Ahab's palace. He had a secular job just the same as most of us. Verse three says he was a devout believer in the Lord. That's a good thing. Consider verse four: "While Jezebel was killing off the LORD's prophets, Obadiah had taken a hundred prophets and hidden them in two caves, fifty in each, and had supplied them with food and water." So, would you say that Obadiah was one of the good guys here? I'd say that Obadiah was certainly a good man but I think the Holy Spirit has included him in the story to show the difference between a good person, who was a believer, and a person filled with the Spirit of God.

In Samaria, a three-year famine would have been very devastating. Many people probably starved to death. What was Ahab, the leader of the people, doing? He and his employee Obadiah were traveling around the drought-devastated country looking for good grazing land for Ahab's own animals. Ahab went in one direction and Obadiah went in another. It seems that Ahab was more concerned about his livestock than he was about his subjects. That tells us much about what kind of king he was.

> As Obadiah was walking along, Elijah met him. Obadiah recognized him, bowed down to the ground, and said, "Is it really you, my lord Elijah?" "Yes," he replied. "Go tell your master, Elijah is here." "What have I done wrong," asked Obadiah, "that you are handing your servant over to Ahab to be put to death? As surely as the LORD your God lives, there is not a nation or kingdom where my master has not sent someone to look for you. And whenever a nation or kingdom claimed you were not there, he made them swear they could not find you."

> (1 Kings 18:7-10)

Notice something significant here. When Obadiah referred to the Lord he said, "The Lord your God." Back in the last chapter when Elijah prayed for the widow's son, he cried out to "The Lord my God."

Obadiah gives us a picture of a good man who meant well and did some good things, but wasn't living in the power of the Spirit. Obadiah was a people pleaser. He cared a lot about what people thought of him. He cared what Ahab thought of him; he cared what Elijah thought of him. Obadiah made sure he got credit for the good things he did. Obadiah was afraid. He was afraid of what his boss would do to him and he was afraid of what the people would think of him. He was a man divided by his fears. Obadiah was trying to live on the fence, one foot in the world and one in the Kingdom.

Many of us live perched on that same fence, wanting to live for God and yet desperately needing the approval of the world around us. We try to find a balance between living godly lives and being "one of the gang" in a fallen culture. We will not find the power of the Holy Spirit while riding this fence.

The Bible tells us: "Do not be yoked together with unbelievers. For what do righteousness and wickedness have in common? Or what fellowship can light have with darkness?" (2 Cor. 6:14). That word "yoked" literally means "mixed together."

What was it about Elijah that made him able to be so used of God? What did Elijah have that Obadiah didn't have? What was the secret of his strength and fearlessness? What can you and I get from this story that we can bring to our own story? How can we be "people who do exploits," like Elijah, instead of people who play it safe and go nowhere like Obadiah. One thousand years later they were still talking about the spirit of Elijah. After this story we never hear of Obadiah again.

What characteristics did Elijah have that allowed God to use him so powerfully? First of all, Elijah was obedient. Remember Elijah's response when the Lord told him to go to Kerith. He obeyed instantly. Elijah was feeling strong and bold and yet the Lord told him to go hide at Kerith. His response was simply: "So he did what the Lord had told him." Then again when the time came for Elijah to leave Kerith the Lord said: "Go at once to Zarephath of Sidon and stay there."

Elijah's response: "So he went to Zarephath." And now in our story, Jehovah speaks once again and Elijah is ready to move as soon as he hears God's marching orders: "Go and present yourself to Ahab, and I will send rain on the land. So Elijah went to present himself to Ahab."

We have plenty of examples of Elijah's obedience to the Lord. Don't think of obedience as obeying some list of rules somewhere. Jesus came to fulfill the law; we no longer live by it. Jesus has given us his Spirit. We need to learn to listen to and obey the voice of the Spirit.

But obedience isn't the bottom line; it never is. How is it that Elijah was obedient and Obadiah wasn't? The bottom line was that Elijah was a man who feared God and Obadiah was a man who feared men. Now it's important that we don't get confused by that word "fear." God doesn't want us to fear him the way we normally define the word. God is our daddy. Good parents would never want their children to be afraid of them. As a young father, I thought that if my children were afraid of discipline they would be good. That concept worked when my children were very young, but as they got older, I realized that fear was a very poor basis for a relationship. I far prefer respect over fear and as it turns out, so does God. In the Bible, the word translated "fear" when talking about how we relate to God literally means "to be in awe of." My dog Rocky demonstrated with amazing clarity today exactly what it means to be obedient. If you know Rocky, you are laughing right now. Naughty is his middle name. But it isn't his willingness to obey the rules that endears him to me. I decided to get a little exercise today so I made a deal with my wife that I would walk to the coffee shop (about a mile) and she would drive there to join me. As I walked out of the yard and headed toward the coffee shop, Rocky followed me to the corner of the yard. We have an underground electric fence so he stopped at the edge of the invisible wire but it was obvious by his riveted attention and wagging tail that he wanted to go along. About an hour-and-a-half later, after spending time at the coffee shop, as Barb and I pulled into the driveway, I noticed

Rocky still sitting in the corner of the yard where he last saw me, waiting. I pulled the car into the driveway, lowered my window and yelled "Rocky, I'm back!" He came running as fast as his Beagle legs would carry him with an obvious expression of joy on his face. He had spent my whole absence expectantly waiting for my return so he could be with me. That is a great picture of what it means to fear (be in awe of) God.

The Bible is filled with examples of men who feared God. In Genesis chapter twenty-two God asked Abraham to take his son Isaac to the top of a mountain and kill him as a sacrifice to the Lord? Abraham was obedient because he trusted God. It was a test, and with Abraham poised with the knife raised over his head, an angel spoke:

> "Do not lay a hand on the boy," he said. "Do not do anything to him. Now I know that you fear God, because you have not withheld from me your son, your only son."
>
> (Gen. 22:12)

There are examples in the Bible of how God's power was able to flow through

Joseph, Moses, and Job, all because they feared (respected, honored, trusted) God. In the New Testament, the Apostle Peter gave us words to live by that articulate the principle:

> Live as free men, but do not use your freedom as a cover-up for evil; live as servants of God. Show proper respect to everyone: Love the brotherhood of believers, fear God, honor the king.
>
> (1 Pet. 2:16-17)

There is one more reason why God's power was able to flow through Elijah and not Obadiah. Obadiah had vision trouble. Because he wasn't filled with God's Spirit, he couldn't see life from God's perspective. He saw danger all around him. Ahab could kill him and his own people could reject him. He was an insecure man with a small god. Elijah, on the other hand, was walking close to God; when God said go, he went, and when God said stay, he stayed. Because he walked close to God, he saw things from God's perspective. This is illustrated so well in the life of Elisha, Elijah's successor:

When the servant of the man of God got up and went out early the next morning, an army with horses and chariots had surrounded the city. "Oh, my lord, what shall we do?" the servant asked. "Don't be afraid," the prophet answered. "Those who are with us are more than those who are with them." And Elisha prayed, "O LORD, open his eyes so he may see." Then the LORD opened the servant's eyes, and he looked and saw the hills full of horses and chariots of fire all around Elisha.

(2 Kings 6:15-17)

Elijah wasn't a man with more character than Obadiah; he wasn't somehow better. What was superior about Elijah wasn't something within him - it was his connection to the living God, Jehovah.

It's easy to be brave when you see life through God's eyes.

The Lord wants us all to see with his eyes. He wants us all to possess the spirit of Elijah, that unconquerable spirit that can do great exploits for God because it has no fear of people. Ask God today for the boldness of a lion. Ask him for vision to see life through his eyes, ask him for the spirit of Elijah! "The righteous are as bold as a lion" (Prov. 28:1). Join the writer of the book of Hebrews today in proclaiming with confidence, "The Lord is my helper; I will not be afraid. What can [people] do to me?" (Heb. 13:6).

The idea that I should please God, not people, has bothered me because it seems like a performance thing, something I just have to somehow generate myself. It seems like I have to just grit my teeth and stop worrying about what others think of me. I know that my trying to make this work is fruitless. But we look to Jesus' to see the reality of pleasing God. He is the benchmark for us, teaching us how to live for God. One story from Luke's gospel makes this clear. As Luke tells the story, Jesus was teaching in one of the synagogues when a woman approached him who had been crippled for eighteen years. She was bent over and couldn't straighten up. When Jesus saw her he had compassion on her and said to her, "Woman, you are set free from your infirmity" (Luke 13:12). When Jesus put his hand on her she was immediately healed and stood upright, praising God. This scene caught the attention of the synagogue ruler who rebuked Jesus in public and said to the people, "There are six days for work, so come and be healed on those days, not on the Sabbath" (Luke 13:14). Jesus responded to the synagogue ruler with boldness:

> You hypocrites! Doesn't each of you on the Sabbath untie his ox or donkey from the stall and lead it out to give it water? Then should not this woman, a daughter of Abraham, whom Satan has kept bound for eighteen long years, be set free on the Sabbath day from what bound her?
>
> (Luke 13:15-16)

What if Jesus had been a people-pleaser? He wouldn't have been able to heal the woman because he would have been afraid he might lose the confidence and approval of the synagogue leader. Being a people-pleaser robs us of our ministry. But Jesus wasn't a people-pleaser...why? It's because he was so secure in His Father's love that He didn't need the approval of others.

And so, this idea of pleasing God rather than people isn't about performance, but rather, about truth. When we know and experience the truth of God's love for us, and see it for how big a love it really is, we will no longer need approval from mere humans. And so, like every other area of my life, God wants to show me the way by showing me himself.

Life Lessons

We need to learn to please only God and not be divided by our fears.

Consider and discuss: Obadiah seemed like a pretty good guy. What's wrong with just trying to do my best?

What are the dangers and opportunities of a secular job?

Describe what it means to you to fear God.

How much do you fear what people think of you? Do you fear people more than you fear God? Do you want to be a person who "does exploits" for God or would you rather just "play it safe"?

Peace characterizes a person who fears God; what characterizes a person who fears man? Which kind of person do you want to be and why?

CHAPTER 10

The Shootout at the OK Carmel!

> So Obadiah went to meet Ahab and told him, and Ahab went to meet Elijah. When he saw Elijah, he said to him, "Is that you, you troubler of Israel?" "I have not made trouble for Israel," Elijah replied. "But you and your father's family have. You have abandoned the LORD's commands and have followed the Baals.
>
> (1 Kings 18: 16-18)

In our story Ahab and Elijah meet again. When they meet, Ahab calls Elijah the "troubler of Israel." Elijah wasn't the first and he certainly wouldn't be the last to be called a troublemaker. In the New Testament, when the Jewish high priest brought charges against the Apostle Paul, he called him a troublemaker: "We have found this man to be a troublemaker, stirring up riots among the Jews all over the world. He is a ringleader of the Nazarene sect" (Acts 24:5). The Hebrew word Ahab used literally means "to roil" or stir things up. Ahab was accusing Elijah of rocking the boat, of stirring things up, of clouding the truth. An analogy can be made from the way wine was made. They would let wine sit in casks and as the sediment settled to the bottom they carefully poured off the pure wine. If the wine was stirred, the result would be a cloudy liquid filled with impurities. A "troubler" stirs up the sediment so truth and purity are always clouded with the filter of personal ethics. Ahab accused Elijah of stirring things up, of spreading untruths about Baal, of bad-mouthing his god.

Elijah's response: "I have not made trouble for Israel," Elijah replied. "But you and your father's family have. You have abandoned the LORD's commands and have followed

116

the Baals" (1 Kings 18:18). Elijah boldly turned the argument back on Ahab. He said, "You are the one clouding the truth."

And so the battle lines are drawn. It's not about strength. It's not about power. It's a battle for truth. Who is God? Is the Lord God, or is Baal? That battle for truth is the same battle that we wage with our enemy today. Today we live in the middle of this battle for truth but we don't actually fight. As a matter of fact, we are the battlefield. The battle is in our minds, and the one we believe, wins. God is the God of truth and Satan is the father of lies. The one we listen to and believe wins the battle for our lives.

Truth is our great liberator. When we believe the truth we are free. When we believe a lie we are in bondage. The question for us is, "Who will we believe and who will we give our devotion to?"

So it's a battle for what is true. Elijah is ready. He proposes a test. Is Baal god, or the Lord?

> Now summon the people from all over Israel to meet me on Mount Carmel. And bring the four hundred and fifty prophets

of Baal and the four hundred prophets of Asherah, who eat at Jezebel's table." So Ahab sent word throughout all Israel and assembled the prophets on Mount Carmel.

(1 Kings 18:19-20)

Breaking News: Elijah's back! Elijah and Ahab meet at OK Carmel for shootout!

How long do you think it might have taken for the word to be spread to all of Israel, to gather everyone who would come and to assemble all the false prophets? What do you think Elijah might have been doing during this time? What would you be doing before your greatest challenge; a battle that would shape the rest of your life; a life that may be rather short if God doesn't come through? Imagine the scene as the mob assembles. I picture Elijah and the prophets of Baal standing on a promontory with thousands of Israelites below with upturned faces. The north and east side of Mount Carmel were steep cliffs, but the south and west sides had landscapes flowing down toward the Mediterranean; thus, the people probably all gathered on that half circle below.

Imagine Elijah facing that crowd and with a loud voice he declared:

> How long will you waver between two opinions? If the LORD is God, follow him; but if Baal is God, follow him. But the people said nothing.

(1 Kings 18:21)

"The people said nothing." What do you suppose the people were thinking? The god Baal was thought to be the god of nature. There were actually several gods they worshipped, but chief among them was the storm god Baal. They believed that Baal controlled the weather and could bless them by making it rain or curse them by bringing drought. The Israelites had been worshippers of Jehovah, but they were also farmers. The temptation to supplement Jehovah by also appealing to Baal had proven just too much for them. For many years they had combined their worship of Jehovah with their worship of Baal. Now Jehovah worship was on the way out as Baal worship was threatening a complete takeover. Elijah told them that they couldn't sit on the fence where God was concerned; was the Lord their God, or was Baal? They couldn't have it two ways. Elijah told the people that they could no longer dance between these two gods. They were going to have to choose. "If Baal is god, follow him; if the Lord is God, then follow him." All of this trouble stemmed from the fact that the Israelites weren't willing to trust God to meet all their needs. They felt like they needed to help him out by supplementing with other gods. They "danced" between these two gods, like a man divided. What about us? I've never met a Baal worshipper. How does all of this apply to us? Ask yourself what or who shares your devotion with Jesus. The Lord tells us-

> No one can serve two masters. Either he will hate the one and love the other, or he will be devoted to the one and despise the other. You cannot serve both God and money.
>
> (Matt. 6:24)
>
> You cannot drink the cup of the Lord and the cup of demons too; you cannot have a part in both the Lord's table and the table of demons.
>
> (1 Cor. 10:21)

> Do not be yoked together with unbelievers. For what do righteousness and wickedness have in common? Or what fellowship can light have with darkness?

> (2 Cor. 6:14)

What gods share your loyalty with Jehovah? What do you dance with that distracts you from relying on God? What relationship, skill, position, or possession do you put before God? Are you dancing? Are you trying to win the approval of people and at the same time the "well-done" of your Master-Planner, Jesus Christ? This is a lot to think about. "But the people said nothing."

The Shootout:

Then Elijah said to them:

> I am the only one of the LORD's prophets left, but Baal has four hundred and fifty prophets. Get two bulls for us. Let them choose one for themselves, and let them cut it into pieces and put it on the wood but not set fire to it. I will prepare the other bull and put it on the wood but not set fire to it. Then you call on the name of your god, and I will call on the name of

the LORD. The god who answers by fire—
he is God. Then all the people said,
"What you say is good."

(1 Kings 18:22-24)

"The god who answers by fire—he is God."
Elijah made them an offer they couldn't
refuse. Baal was the storm god and also the
god of fire! But fire was also an emblem of
Jehovah. In the Bible, "fire" symbolizes the
glory of the Lord. "To the Israelites, the
glory of the LORD looked like a consuming
fire on top of the mountain." (Ex. 24:17).
Fire was the way God manifested himself to
Moses at the burning bush. And there were
tongues of fire that appeared above the
disciples of Jesus in the upper room after
Jesus' crucifixion. Before Pentecost, the
disciples fled from their enemies. But at
Pentecost, they were given a holy boldness
that changed their lives forever. Jesus had
promised them the presence of God as
manifested by the Holy Spirit:

> But you will receive power when the Holy
> Spirit comes on you; and you will be my
> witnesses in Jerusalem, and in all Judea
> and Samaria, and to the ends of the
> earth.

(Acts 1:8)

In that upper room they were praying for the Holy Spirit as Jesus had promised.

> When the day of Pentecost came, they were all together in one place. Suddenly a sound like the blowing of a violent wind came from heaven and filled the whole house where they were sitting. They saw what seemed to be tongues of fire that separated and came to rest on each of them. All of them were filled with the Holy Spirit and began to speak in other tongues as the Spirit enabled them.

(Acts 2:1-4)

Wow! Fire came to be the symbol of God's empowering presence. Elijah had given the prophets of Baal a challenge they couldn't resist.

Game on! The prophets of Baal went first:

> So they took the bull given them and prepared it. Then they called on the name of Baal from morning till noon. "O Baal, answer us!" they shouted. But there was no response; no one answered. And they danced around the altar they had made.

(1 Kings 18:26)

They danced around the altar until noon. Noon was a significant time. That was when Baal supposedly would be strongest.

> At noon Elijah began to taunt them. "Shout louder!" he said. "Surely he is a god! Perhaps he is deep in thought, or busy, or traveling. Maybe he is sleeping and must be awakened."

(Verse 27)

I'm not so sure we should be taunting our enemies. Maybe Elijah was being a little naughty. Maybe Jehovah smiled.

> So they shouted louder and slashed themselves with swords and spears, as was their custom, until their blood flowed.

(Verse 28)

Notice that the prophets of Baal were very passionate about what they believed. You can tell who or what your god is by what you are passionate about.

> Midday passed, and they continued their frantic prophesying until the time for the evening sacrifice. But there was no

response, no one answered; no one paid attention.

(Verse 29)

"Midday passed." How sad for the lost all around us who are passionate toward the wrong things. There are many today who try and try and never come to peace because their gods have let them down. Aren't you glad that followers of Jesus don't have to wait until noon for our God to be strong!

> Then Elijah said to all the people, "Come here to me." They came to him, and he repaired the altar of the LORD, which was in ruins. Elijah took twelve stones, one for each of the tribes descended from Jacob, to whom the word of the LORD had come, saying, "Your name shall be Israel."

(1 Kings 18:30-31)

"Come here to me." The crowd squeezed closer with every eye wide open. He wanted them to see that what was about to happen was not a trick! He chose twelve stones, one for each of the tribes of Israel. The nation had been divided and fractured for many years over a dispute about which god they would follow. Since the days of Jeroboam's calves, the nation had not been unified around the one true God. Elijah chose twelve stones to signify that before this day was done all Israel would worship Jehovah. "Your name shall be Israel."

> With the stones he built an altar in the name of the LORD, and he dug a trench around it large enough to hold two seahs of seed. He arranged the wood, cut the bull into pieces and laid it on the wood. Then he said to them, "Fill four large jars with water and pour it on the offering and on the wood." "Do it again," he said, and they did it again. "Do it a third time," he ordered, and they did it the third time. The water ran down around the altar and even filled the trench.
>
> (1 Kings 18:32-35)

Why make it so hard with all that water? The Israelites had tried to make it easier for God, helping him out with the weather by combining Baal worship with the true worship of Jehovah. Their god was too small to take care of them on his own. Elijah was about to expand their perception of Jehovah God. That raises a question for us. How big is your God? What action do you take in your life that is supposed to be a matter of faith? If we are going to be like Elijah and do exploits for God, we will need to learn the attitude of heart that God had taught him.

The key to Elijah's heart is revealed in his prayer in verse 36:

> At the time of sacrifice, the prophet Elijah stepped forward and prayed: "O LORD, God of Abraham, Isaac and Israel, let it be known today that you are God in Israel and that I am your servant and have done all these things at your command. Let it be known today that you are God in Israel."

Do you hear the passion in those words? Elijah's prayer is the key to his heart. He had come to the place in his life where he thought more about what the people thought of God than of him. He had given up his own interests and adopted the interests of Jehovah.

"...and that I am your servant"

He considered himself a servant. A slave or servant doesn't originate plans, but seeks the master's will. Elijah had come to the attitude of heart where he was plastic in his masters hands. Sometimes I think that we are way too quick to get busy for God. We decide what we will do for God and then we go off and do it without first inquiring if this is what he wants us to do; we don't recognize his absolute ownership.

"...and have done all these things at your command."

Elijah was eager to be in the center of God's will and work God's plan. When a person is working God's plan, he is invincible.

This story is all about you and me. It's all about becoming the people of God. It's all about believing him and worshipping only him. It's all about giving our lives to him. When Elijah prayed and asked God to answer him so that "these people will know that you, O LORD, are God, and that you are turning their hearts back again," he was talking about you and me. The Lord has given us this story so that we can make it our story. We might as well be standing on the slopes of Mount Carmel looking up at the prophet as he asks us, "How long will you waver between two opinions? If the

LORD is God, follow him; but if Baal is God, follow him."

"Answer me, O LORD; answer me, so these people will know that you, O LORD, are God and that you are turning their hearts back to yourself." Here you have Elijah's pure motive. When the Lord brings you and me to the place in our lives where we care this much about the things that God cares about, then John 15:7-8 becomes reality for us- "If you remain in me and my words remain in you, ask whatever you wish, and it will be given you. This is to my Father's glory, that you bear much fruit, showing yourselves to be my disciples."

> Then the fire of the LORD fell and burned up the sacrifice, the wood, the stones and the soil, and also licked up the water in the trench. When all the people saw this, they fell prostrate and cried, "The LORD-- he is God! The LORD-- he is God!"

> (1 Kings 18:38-39)

Elijah was able to call down the fire from heaven because he knew the will of the father and he cooperated with it in his life.

His motive was not that the people would see what a great prophet he was, but that they would see how great God is. God will use any of us who are willing to be a channel of his power and love, anyone who will connect with his purposes, and put his purposes before their own.

The shootout at the OK Carmel...no contest!

Life Lessons

You can tell who or what your god is by what you are passionate about.

_____

Consider and discuss: What "two opinions" do you waver between? Are you trying to win the approval of the world and at the same time the "well-done" of your Master-Planner, Jesus Christ? Name the things in your life that compete with God for your devotion and attention?

What are you passionate about? What person or thing do you spend your time thinking about to the exclusion of Jesus?

Is it the passion of your life that your family, friends, and co-workers will know that he is God?

John 15:5-8

James 1:1-4

Lessons.

1. Follow God

2. FAITH

CHAPTER 11

Lessons from Carmel

What do we need in order for our lives to be a channel of blessing? What do we need to be a part of Jehovah's plan to turn the hearts of the people of our time back to him? How can we have the "spirit of Elijah?"

1. We need to learn to rest in God's provision as at Kerith, to be dependent on him.

2. We need to learn humility as Elijah did at Zarephath.

3. We need to learn to be more in awe of God than men as negatively illustrated by Obadiah.

4. We need to come to our Carmel where we place ourselves on the altar of sacrifice.

5. We need to be in the place of unity with our brothers and sisters as represented by the altar of twelve stones.

The wood was on the altar to help the sacrifice burn. The wood represents our ministry. Our ministry is what helps us burn bright as Christians. We must give our ministry to Jesus. He must be the conductor. "Lord, I give you all I do."

Next there was the sacrifice. The bull represents us. We must place ourselves on the altar of sacrifice. "Lord, I give you all I am."

Then there was the water. The water represents baptism, where we die to self. This is where we lay all our self-effort at the foot of the cross...no more trying, only trusting. "Lord, I give you all I do and all I am."

The fire represents passion from heaven. When the fire falls, we are set aflame with God's passion and purified with His desires. We don't light the fire; we place ourselves on the altar of sacrifice. We give God all that we do and all that we are, and then...

Then we call out to him: "O Lord, - let it be known today that you are God in Israel..., answer me, O Lord, answer me, so these people will know that you, O Lord, are God, and that you are turning their hearts back again." Then your life is set on fire for the Kingdom of God. Then the world will know that the Lord, He is God!

Is that what you want for your life?

> Then Elijah commanded them, "Seize the prophets of Baal. Don't let anyone get away!" They seized them, and Elijah had them brought down to the Kishon Valley and slaughtered there.
>
> (1 Kings 18:40)

Was this the right thing to do?

> If a prophet, or one who foretells by dreams, appears among you and announces to you a miraculous sign or wonder, and if the sign or wonder of

which he has spoken takes place, and he says, "Let us follow other gods" (gods you have not known) "and let us worship them," you must not listen to the words of that prophet or dreamer. The LORD your God is testing you to find out whether you love him with all your heart and with all your soul. It is the LORD your God you must follow, and him you must revere. Keep his commands and obey him; serve him and hold fast to him. That prophet or dreamer must be put to death, because he preached rebellion against the LORD your God, who brought you out of Egypt and redeemed you from the land of slavery; he has tried to turn you from the way the LORD your God commanded you to follow. You must purge the evil from among you.

(Deut. 13:1-5)

Acting on God's authority, Elijah purged the evil from Israel that day. God also wants to purge the evil from our lives. To be filled with the Holy Spirit requires doing away with anything in us that can't cohabit with God's Spirit. Ask God to reveal to you those things that have to go and then ask him to get rid of them for you. He is willing to do the work but he needs your permission.

Life Lessons

Consider and discuss: How is God teaching you to be dependent? How is he teaching you to be humble? Do you know God well enough to be in awe of him?

What lessons have you learned at your Carmel experience? Was it worth it?

What is the next battle God has for you? Will you give him permission to use you? The shootout at the OK Carmel is no contest when God gives the orders; will you let him take the lead in your next adventure?

CHAPTER 12

A Different Kind of Drought

The drought in the land ends. The drought in Elijah's heart begins.

> And Elijah said to Ahab, "Go, eat and drink, for there is the sound of a heavy rain." So Ahab went off to eat and drink, but Elijah climbed to the top of Carmel, bent down to the ground and put his face between his knees. "Go and look toward the sea," he told his servant. And he went up and looked. "There is nothing there," he said. Seven times Elijah said, "Go back." The seventh time the servant reported, "A cloud as small as a man's hand is rising from the sea." So Elijah

said, "Go and tell Ahab, `Hitch up your chariot and go down before the rain stops you.'" Meanwhile, the sky grew black with clouds, the wind rose, a heavy rain came on and Ahab rode off to Jezreel. The power of the LORD came upon Elijah and, tucking his cloak into his belt, he ran ahead of Ahab all the way to Jezreel. Now Ahab told Jezebel everything Elijah had done and how he had killed all the prophets with the sword. So Jezebel sent a messenger to Elijah to say, "May the gods deal with me, be it ever so severely, if by this time tomorrow I do not make your life like that of one of them."

(1 Kings 18:41-19:2)

What gods? An empty threat! Based on what we know about Elijah so far in our story, what would you expect his response would be to Jezebel's threat? His response:

Elijah was afraid and ran for his life. When he came to Beersheba in Judah, he left his servant there, while he himself went a day's journey into the desert. He came to a broom tree, sat down under it and prayed that he might die. "I have had enough, LORD," he said. "Take my life; I am no better than my ancestors."

(1 Kings 19:3-4)

He ran for his life. What is going on with our prophet?

The Apostle Peter had a similar experience. Like Elijah, Peter also lost heart when things got tough. Remember when Jesus came walking across the water to Peter and his friends when they were out in the boat? Having trouble believing that it was Jesus and not a ghost, Peter exclaimed, "Lord, if it's you, tell me to come to you on the water" (Matt. 14:28). Peter got out of the boat and walked on the water toward Jesus. One would think that this experience alone would be enough to quench all doubt from Peter's mind forever; and yet when Peter saw a little wind and the water getting rougher, he lost courage. Beginning to sink, he cried out, "Lord save me."

Why did Peter lose courage when he saw a few waves? Actually, the fact that Peter could even see the waves tells me that he wasn't looking at the Lord. Peter was afraid because he took his eyes off the Lord and only saw the waves.

Up until now, Elijah had displayed amazing courage because he had never lost sight of Jehovah. When Elijah only saw the Lord, he had no fear. As long as he was connected to his source of strength, he had courage. When he began to look at the danger around him instead of God's cause in front of him, he lost courage.

Faith always thrives when God occupies our whole field of vision.

Elijah saw Jezebel's threat instead of the Lord. Also, note that when Elijah ran, he left his servant behind. I don't know if this is significant or not, but I wonder why he left his servant behind. This is the first we've heard about a servant. Why tell us about him now that he's being left behind? Could it be that in his greatest need for someone to be there to support him and to help him process reality in the midst of his fear, that Elijah isolated himself? Is that what you do? Just when you need people the most, you withdraw. How many times have you been down and you just didn't feel like going to church or to that small group? Do you isolate yourself from God's people just when you need them the most? A favorite ploy of the enemy is to divide and conquer.

Ever pray a broom tree prayer? Ever pray "I have had enough, Lord, take my life." If God had taken Elijah at his word, Elijah would have died at the lowest point in his life, would have never heard the still small voice of God, and he would never have founded the school of the prophets. If God had answered Elijah's prayer, Elijah would have never experienced riding to heaven aboard a flaming chariot. Only God knew that Elijah's best days were still ahead of him.

Could it be that your best days are still ahead of you!

God didn't take Elijah at his word. Aren't you glad that God doesn't answer all your prayers? "Take my life; I am no better than my ancestors." Elijah, Elijah! Who ever said that you had to be better than your ancestors or live up to some standard of performance? He was agonizing because he had let God down. He had lost faith in Jehovah just like his ancestors when they began to worship Baal. Where was it written that Elijah had to measure up to some standard before he could be used by God? He was saying that without God he was useless. God already knew that! Are you fit to be used by God? Are you worthy? Maybe those are the wrong questions? Are you willing?

> Then he laid down under the tree and fell asleep. All at once an angel touched him and said, "Get up and eat." He looked around, and there by his head was a cake of bread baked over hot coals, and a jar of water. He ate and drank and then lay down again.
>
> (1 Kings 19:5-6)

When we are walking with the Lord, it's not difficult to believe that God loves us. But when we are not where we are supposed to be, when we are not trusting, not following, not keeping step with the Spirit, it's then that we find it hard to believe that his love for us is constant, that it never wavers, and that there is nothing that we can do that will separate us from the love of God.

Life Lessons

Faith always thrives when God occupies our whole field of vision.

Consider and discuss: Can you think of a time when your faith failed because you started looking at your circumstance instead of Jesus?

Do you tend to isolate yourself from God's people when you are depressed or discouraged?

What have you learned from this chapter that will help you face your enemy head on and with the truth of God's Word?

CHAPTER 13

Walking Away From Jesus

So how does God feel about us when we are not following him? Maybe you've not been walking with the Lord and you are not sure how God feels about you right now. If that is you then please pay close attention to Peter's story. When Jesus commissioned Peter into service, what did he tell him to do?

> As Jesus was walking beside the Sea of Galilee, he saw two brothers, Simon called Peter and his brother, Andrew. They were casting a net into the lake, for they were fishermen. "Come, follow me,"

Jesus said, "and I will make you fishers of men."

(Matt. 4:18-19)

In Peter's story, Jesus has been crucified and resurrected. Peter knows Jesus is alive but his relationship with Jesus just doesn't seem the same as it used to be. Peter doesn't sit constantly at his Master's feet anymore. The cock has crowed 3 times. Peter has let his master down. Now, in his resurrected body, Jesus only appears in public, and even less and less. Peter wonders what the future holds. They were three wonderful years, but are they over? Where to from here? The glow is off his life. This is a story of a man who, after following Jesus, after receiving his commission to fish for men, got discouraged and went back to his old way of life. Notice Jesus' reaction to all of this, because this is the way Jesus reacts to us when we slip back and need to be rebuked and corrected. If you have slipped backward a bit in your walk with the Master and wonder if He is angry with you, then this story is for you!

> Afterward Jesus appeared again to his disciples, by the Sea of Tiberias. It happened this way: Simon Peter, Thomas (called Didymus), Nathanael from Cana in Galilee, the sons of Zebedee, and two other disciples were together. "I'm going out to fish," Simon Peter told them, and they said, "We'll go with you." So they went out and got into the boat, but that night they caught nothing.

> (John 21:1-3)

Peter was a fisherman. Jesus had changed his life and given him a new calling. He was now to be a fisher of men. Peter was a rough hulk of a man, and like many strong men, he had a bent toward self-sufficiency. He was accustomed to taking care of himself. Even after spending over three years with Jesus he still had this independent streak. "You yourselves know that these hands of mine [Peter] have supplied my own needs and the needs of my companions" (Acts 20:34). This verse is out of context and Peter was a changed man by this time, but you can see that it was difficult for him to rely on the Lord. He was the kind of man who was used to meeting his own needs, taking care of himself and others.

Now, after Jesus' resurrection, those three years seemed like a dream to Peter and he reverted to his old ways. He went fishing. Instead of following Jesus, who had given him direction for three years, he retreated to his safety zone where he was most comfortable. Not only did Peter revert to old ways, but he brought his friends with him, causing them to stumble in their walk with Jesus. How will Jesus respond, knowing that his No.1 man had abandoned the cause?

> Early in the morning, Jesus stood on the shore, but the disciples did not realize that it was Jesus. He called out to them, "Friends, haven't you any fish?" "No," they answered.

> (John 21:4-5)

Jesus called out to them as "friends" but the disciples didn't realize that it was him. "Do you have any fish?" he asked. Did Jesus rebuke them for going backward in their walk with him? Was he angry? - Did he say, "What's the matter with you blockheads? Didn't you learned anything in those three years I have spent with you? I'm disgusted with all of you, and especially you, Peter. You're supposed to be a leader and you are leading my sheep astray!" No, Jesus didn't rebuke them. He simply helped them see that their efforts at finding satisfaction apart from him were fruitless. He simply said, "How's the fishing?" They just looked at each other with that look common to all fishermen when they've been skunked.

Jesus then gave them a suggestion:

> He said, "Throw your net on the right side of the boat and you will find some." When they did, they were unable to haul the net in because of the large number of fish.

> (John 21:6)

So we have Jesus the carpenter telling Peter the fisherman how to catch fish. Amazingly, Peter responds:

> Master, we've worked hard all night and haven't caught anything. But because you say so, I will let down the nets.

> (Luke 5:5)

When they let down the nets they caught a huge catch of fish. When they recognized that it was Jesus standing on the shore, Peter jumped into the water and swam to greet Jesus. Jesus had a fire going and was fixing breakfast for Peter and the other men. It was a glad reunion, but I can't help but wonder what was going on in Peter's mind. He knew that Jesus' plan for him was to proclaim the gospel. His new calling was fishing for men. I can imagine Peter waiting for those words of rebuke from Jesus. He was expecting Jesus to say, "Why are you fishing Peter?" What Jesus did say on the beach that morning tells us so much about how Jesus deals with his children who have slipped away.

> When they had finished eating, Jesus said to Simon Peter, "Simon son of John, do you truly love [agape] me more than these?" "Yes, Lord," he said, "you know that I love [phileo] you." Jesus said, "Feed my lambs."

> (John 21:15)

Jesus asked Peter if he loved him with God's unconditional (agape) love. And he compared Peter's love for him to the old way of life with the words "more than these." Peter was cut by those words and they played back in his head; do I have complete unconditional love for Jesus, he thought? Peter didn't know how to answer. He stammered as he said, "You know that I have affection (phileo) for you." Jesus' response to that was, "Feed my sheep."

> Again Jesus said, "Simon, son of John, do you truly love [agape] me?" He answered, "Yes, Lord, you know that I love [phileo] you." Jesus said, "Take care of my sheep."
>
> (John 21:16)

Jesus asked the question again, but this time he dropped the comparison "more than these", moving closer to Peter. Peter still didn't know what to do with that word "agape" which means unconditional love. It must have sounded pitiful, even to Peter, as he forced out, "Yes, Jesus, you know that I like you a lot." Jesus responded: "Take care of my sheep."

> The third time he said to him, "Simon son of John, do you love [phileo] me?" Peter was hurt because Jesus asked him the third time, "Do you love [phileo] me?"

153

He said, "Lord, you know all things; you know that I love [phileo] you." Jesus said, "Feed my sheep."

(John 21:17).

In their conversation, Jesus has moved all the way to Peter. He is no longer asking if Peter has unconditional love for him; he is now saying, "Peter, do you truly have affection for me?" Jesus has rephrased his question three times, each time moving toward the place where Peter could respond to him.

Jesus does the same with you and me. He is willing to gently meet us where we are, to reach down with a gentle hand. He is ready to lift us up and restore us. Jesus is seeking fellowship with you today and he is willing to come down to where you are and meet you there. He will meet you where you are and gently lift you. You don't need to reach for Jesus. He's right there. Just place your hand in his and he will lift you. Jesus' intent was not to rebuke Peter but to gently restore him. With the words, "feed my sheep," Peter was re-commissioned with God's plan for his life. When Jesus and

Peter said goodbye that day, Jesus leaned toward Peter and whispered in his ear, "Follow me." Peter was re-fitted, re-commissioned and ready for Pentecost. After that time on the beach, Peter preached a sermon and three thousand came to know the Lord. Are you ready to meet Jesus on the beach today?

Elijah reminds me a lot of Peter; two independent men who were always tempted to "fix" things themselves. Many of us men struggle with the need to grab life by the throat and take care of business. While not necessarily a bad trait, it makes it difficult for us to handle failure. I've struggled with this myself and I've known many men in particular who are crushed by failure.

Elijah had experienced his greatest conquest, but now found himself locked in a battle with fear. The ravens fed him at Kerith, the widow fed him at Zarephath, but in the pit, in the depths of depression and failure, God sent his angel to feed him. God wasn't mad at Elijah; he saw the failure of Elijah's faith as a need, and dispatched an angel to minister to him. If you are living amongst the wreckage of what might have been your life, take heart! "Why are you downcast, O my soul? Why so disturbed within me? Put your hope in God, for I will yet praise him, my Savior and my God" (Ps. 43:5). God loves to come along side of the downcast and broken hearted. He is the God of new beginnings.

> The angel of the LORD came back a second time and touched him and said, "Get up and eat, for the journey is too much for you." So he got up and ate and drank. Strengthened by that food, he traveled forty days and forty nights until he reached Horeb, the mountain of God.
>
> (1 Kings 19:7-8)

On the strength of that one meal he travelled forty days. Do you want some of that food? Jesus said, "I have food to eat that you know nothing about" (John 4:32). He is the Bread of Life.

Life Lessons

God loves to come along side of the downcast and broken hearted. He is the God of new beginnings.

Consider and discuss: How has this chapter changed your view of the Shepherd and his wayward lambs?

Think of a time when you failed to follow Jesus. In that circumstance did you have a time with the Lord where Jesus ministered to you?

Look for the Gentle Shepherd in the Psalms and in Jesus' own words. In the midst of our pain and misery, he is waiting for us to come to him for a word of hope.

CHAPTER 14

Poor-Poor-Pitiful Me

There he went into a cave and spent the night. And the word of the Lord came to him: "What are you doing here, Elijah?" He replied, "I have been very zealous for the Lord God Almighty. The Israelites have rejected your covenant, broken down your altars, and put your prophets to death with the sword. I am the only one left, and now they are trying to kill me too."

(1 Kings 19:9-10)

Do you ever feel like Elijah? "I am the only one left." Do you ever feel like you are the last one standing? Do you ever feel like everyone else is gone and there is nothing left to do but turn off the lights when you leave? "God, it's just me. I am all alone." Do you ever feel like Elijah? Let's be honest. From time-to-time we all descend into the blue funk of self-pity. We've all played that tune. You and I may occasionally succumb to this, that's not surprising. What is surprising is that even the great prophet Elijah sinks into the same sucking quicksand.

What has happened to our prophet? All his life God has been preparing him. Jehovah has taught Elijah the lessons of humility and of relying on God for his strength. He has taught the prophet the lessons of listening for God's voice and only moving when God says move. God has been preparing him for that climactic showdown on Mount Carmel with the 850 prophets of the false gods. Elijah fulfills his destiny and defeats all the prophets of Baal. Victory! Can you imagine accomplishing the very thing that God has destined you for? Can you imagine the high that Elijah felt as he stood up for God with all of Israel watching? It was the pinnacle of Elijah's life. Now, it's forty days later and the towering giant of a man has descended into poor, poor, pitiful me.

What happened? What happened to our prophet? How did he go from being the man God created him to be to the murky dark waters of self-pity and doubt? One word...*Jezebel*! Remember her words in verse two: "May the gods deal with me, be it ever so severely, if by this time tomorrow I do not make your life like that of one of them." Her gods were not real but her threat was. Jezebel was the wicked queen of Israel, who had all the resources of the throne. When Jezebel learned that her prophets had all been single-handedly slaughtered by the prophet of God, she cursed the God of Israel and threatened to do to Elijah what he had done to all of her prophets. How did Elijah respond? He snapped. The great prophet of God crumbled. The great reformer of Israel ran for his life. God didn't tell him to run. All of these years Elijah has been a man that God could use for one simple reason. Elijah was a man that God could count on to do his will. When God said "Go", Elijah went.

When God said "Stay", Elijah stayed. God could use Elijah because Elijah heard God's voice and he obeyed.

Now here is our great man of God, our prophet of prophets, and he doesn't hear one word from God and yet he runs and runs and runs because he broke. Elijah runs for forty days. Hey, forty days isn't so long. Some of us have been running for much longer than that.

> There he went into a cave and spent the night. And the word of the Lord came to him: What are you doing here, Elijah?
>
> (1 Kings 19:9)

I want you to hang on those words, "What are you doing here?" God may be asking you that same question today. Listen to the prophet's answer:

> He replied, "I have been very zealous for the Lord God Almighty. The Israelites have rejected your covenant, broken down your altars, and put your prophets to death with the sword. I am the only one left, and now they are trying to kill me too."
>
> (1 Kings 19:10)

Welcome to the whining whimper of self-pity. Who of us hasn't succumbed to it? I've been there more times than I care to admit. It's a dark place; a negative poor-poor-me kind of thinking. I've been walking with the Lord for a long time. I know that there is a solution to the blue funk. I know that a heavenly lap is available for me and a daddy who will take my troubles. I know that no matter what state I'm in, Jesus is always willing to stoop to wherever I am and meet me there. That is the great thing about Jesus. He is not far away. He is always close and always available. Even if you are in a place out of his will, even if you are not following his lead in your life, even if you are living in sin, God will find you there, and if you will follow him, he will lead you out.

I know all of that, and yet when I find myself going through a time of self-doubt and self-pity, I struggle to get on top of it. I unload on God. I search for the lap of God and it's like he is playing hide-and-seek with me in the dark. When I find myself in that place, I want out and I want to learn so that I can avoid that "dark damp dungeon" in the future. So I seek God and cry out, "Show me the way out of this dark hole, Lord." I found myself in this place recently and you will never going to guess what the Lord showed me. It was certainly not what I expected. God never fails to surprise me. The more I know about God the more I realize how little I know, and yet in it all, I grow closer to him. What I expected from Jesus was comfort. That's what I prayed for. That's what I hoped for. That's what I thought I needed. But what I got from Jesus wasn't comfort. Somehow, I didn't sense the comforting voice of my Savior. I cried out to him, "Come on God, I'm hurting here. I need your lap. I need your comfort. It's me, God. It's Bob. You know, poor-poor-pitiful me. Come on God. A little sympathy would be nice. I could use a little word of encouragement here."

No, I got the same word from the Lord that Elijah did in his melt-down, "What are you doing here?"

Friends, let me give joyful testimony. On the other side of the blue funk I realize that once again I have been sucked into the devil's trap of self-pity. Satan is the author of self-pity. He designed it just for you and just for me. Why is self-pity designed by Satan? What is so evil about a little self-pity? Friends, I'll tell you, self-pity obliterates God and puts self-interest on the throne. Self-pity makes it all about me. It's SELF-pity.

Do you recognize that sin? It's the same sin that Satan himself committed; it got him kicked out of heaven, and it is his plan for you and me. The Devil doesn't care if you are filled with pride, as he was, or self-pity. Either way, you make it all about you and push God to the background. That is sin!

So God's response to Elijah was, "Hey Elijah, what are you doing here?" Look again at Elijah's response:

> I have been very zealous for the Lord God Almighty. The Israelites have rejected your covenant, broken down your altars, and put your prophets to death with the sword. I am the only one left, and now they are trying to kill me too.
>
> (1 Kings 19:10)

It might sound like Elijah was making it all about God, "...your altar, your prophets, your covenant," but don't you believe it for a minute. Elijah wasn't really saying "it's about you, you, you God." He was saying "it's all about me, me, me."

Maybe you are in a similar frame of mind today. Maybe you are tempted to feel a little hopeless right now. Let me encourage you. The dark, blue funk of hopelessness is but a hair's breadth away from victory. What! Victory? Yes, victory. You might be saying- "But victory seems so far off that the other end of this tunnel reveals nothing but black. I can't even see the road ahead." Let me give you one little statement. If you get nothing more from this chapter, you will go away rich. Get this:

Never are you closer to victory than when you feel completely helpless and realize your only hope is God.

Why is that true? It's true because when we come to the end of ourselves we come to the end of our impotent natural abilities and that is the place where our Savior's unlimited supernatural abilities begin. God only starts where we leave off. When your natural strivings cease and his supernatural strength takes over, then his power will characterize your life.

Life Lessons

Never are you closer to victory than when you feel completely helpless and realize your only hope is God.

Consider and discuss: Make a list of why you feel hopeless today. It's okay to express your negative feelings. As you put your pondering to paper, whether your list be short or long, thank God that he is all you need! He is your source, your strength, your focus, your only hope. Remember, you know the father's heart and you will yet praise him.

Express in prayer this verse: "O our God, We do not know what to do, but our eyes are upon you" (2 Chron. 20:12).

Victory is just over the horizon of praise.

CHAPTER 15

A Redirected Life

"What are you doing here, Elijah?"

The Lord said, "Go out and stand on the mountain in the presence of the Lord, for the Lord is about to pass by." Then a great and powerful wind tore the mountains apart and shattered the rocks before the Lord, but the Lord was not in the wind. After the wind there was an earthquake, but the Lord was not in the earthquake. After the earthquake came a fire, but the Lord was not in the fire. And after the fire came a gentle whisper. When Elijah heard it, he pulled his cloak over his face and went out and stood at the mouth of the cave.

(1 Kings 19:11-13)

Elijah is in a cave. It was on the mountain of God, which is Mount Sinai. Moses may have stood in the same "cleft in the rock" when he encountered God on the mountain. Why is Elijah here? It's simple. He went to the same place where Moses saw God because he was seeking God. "Where are you God?" was the cry of Elijah's heart. "I need you God." Have you ever cried that prayer?

Can you hear Elijah's prayer in that cave, crying out with sobbing voice and wet eyes? "O God, I have been very zealous for you. I have been there when you did your mighty miracles. I was there when you struck fear into the heart of Ahab. I was there when the vessel of oil never went empty and when you raised the widow's son from the dead. I was there when you called down fire from heaven and consumed the sacrifice. But where are you now, Lord? I am here. I am at the same place where you showed yourself to Moses. Show yourself to me. I have seen your glory, now show me yourself."

Elijah had seen the mighty miracles of God. He had seen the power of God defeat his enemies. This was the God he knew. This was the God he expected.

Then the wind started to blow.

Elijah thought to himself, here he comes. Now the power of God will manifest itself and I will go from this place filled up with God. I will blow Jezebel away. But God was not in the wind.

Then came a great earthquake and the mountain shook.

Surely this is him, the prophet thought to himself. God has the power to move mountains and with that power I will devastate my enemies. No more fear! But God was not in the earthquake.

Then the fire came.

Okay, here we go! Fire fell from heaven on Mount Carmel and now Mount Sinai. Fire is the symbol of the manifest presence of God. Remember the burning bush? Surely the presence of the Lord will manifest itself now. You guessed it. The Lord was not in the fire.

Finally there was a gentle whisper.

It was a hushed, quiet whisper. When he strained to hear, I believe the prophet heard the same words once again: "Elijah, what are you doing here?" The gentle voice and calm word from the Lord quieted the prophet. "Lord, I'm all alone," he sobbed. "There are no others that are for you." I believe the Lord answered, "No Elijah, you are wrong."

> Yet I reserve seven thousand in Israel — all whose knees have not bowed down to Baal and all whose mouths have not kissed him.
>
> (1 Kings 19:18)

Maybe in that quiet, calm voice the Lord said, "You are wrong Elijah. You are not alone. I am with you and there are still seven thousand in Israel who need to hear my voice, seven thousand who have not bowed to Baal; seven thousand who you need to talk to about me. What are you doing here Elijah?"

By the way, that is exactly Paul's point when he inserts Elijah's story into his letter to the Romans:

> God did not reject his people, whom he foreknew. Don't you know what the Scripture says in the passage about Elijah — how he appealed to God against Israel: "Lord, they have killed your prophets and torn down your altars; I am the only one left, and they are trying to kill me"? And what was God's answer to him? "I have reserved for myself seven thousand who have not bowed the knee to Baal." So, too, at the present time there is a remnant chosen by grace.
>
> (Rom. 11:2-5)

What was God saying to Elijah, Paul, and us? In a world that looks dark and pagan and lost, God declares for himself a remnant. And so, God presents us with the same question: "What are you doing here? What are you doing in this dark cave of funk?" Maybe he is asking you today, "What are you doing here? What are you doing in the negative, self-defeating dark hole of self-pity? I am not through with you yet and you are not alone. I have a remnant of those who have yet to bow to this world's evil system. I have many who will not hear my voice unless you first hear it." Some of you may be in Elijah's dark cave today. Please don't give up. God is not done with you yet. He is as near to you now as he has ever been, and he wants to reach seven-thousand more through your life.

You say, "Hold it one minute Bob! Don't tell me that God wants to reach seven-thousand souls through my ministry. Come on now, I may not even make it until payday." How can that happen? I'll show you! One more passage of Scripture and I'll show you how it works.

You've heard of the Mount of Transfiguration:

> After six days Jesus took with him Peter, James and John the brother of James, and led them up a high mountain by themselves. There he was transfigured before them. His face shone like the sun, and his clothes became as white as the light. Just then there appeared before them Moses and Elijah, talking with Jesus.
>
> (Matt. 17:1-3)

I have two questions for us to consider about this scene.

1. Why were Moses and Elijah there?

2. What were Jesus, Elijah, and Moses talking about?

Why were Moses and Elijah there? I don't think it is any coincidence that Moses and Elijah shared a very important experience. Both of them melted-down right at the time of their greatest challenge. Moses melted-down and failed just at that climactic moment when the nation of Israel was finally poised to cross over into the land that God had promised them. All of Moses' life was preparation for that moment, and at that moment, he lost it. Elijah had just come from Mt. Carmel, just had his climactic moment, when he lost it. Two men, both mightily used by God, both at the moment of their greatest achievement for God, lost it and descended into the bottomless pit of self-pity. The fact that they both stood on that Mount of Transfiguration with Jesus is testimony to the grace, tenderness and love of a Savior God who never gives up, even though sometimes we do.

What were Moses, Elijah, and Jesus talking about? Jesus was soon to go to Jerusalem where he would be crucified. Don't ever forget that Jesus was fully human and his emotions would be no different than yours or mine. His dread of what lay before him was real and it was heavy. I can imagine Jesus on that mountain, sharing with the two men in the universe who could, more than any others, understand how he must be feeling; the dread in his heart for the days ahead. The two prophets have been through the dark pit of self-pity. They have seen the loving redemption; they have heard that still small voice. I can almost hear them encouraging Jesus. "Just hang on Jesus. You know the father. Don't let your heart be troubled. You will yet praise him" (see Ps. 42-43). Moses and Elijah were there to encourage Jesus. Jesus is here today to encourage you and me. We can do it because he is with us.

He wants you and me to reach our seven-thousand with the message of the quiet whisper.

There was the mighty wind, the earthquake, and the consuming fire, all demonstrating the might and the power of Almighty God! But God's presence was found in a gentle whisper. God was telling Elijah not to concern himself with Jezebel and her empty threats. God was more interested in Elijah and changing him into the person he created him to be. God wanted Elijah to just follow him, to hear his voice and respond.

Is God asking you this question today? "What are you doing here?" Is he asking you why you are in the place you are spiritually? Are you in the place of trust, going when God says go, staying when he says stay?

Let God gentle and quiet you so you can hear even a whisper and run with just one word.

At least six years went by after the Mount Carmel experience before we hear from Elijah again. I don't know if Elijah was busy for Jehovah or if he was on the shelf, waiting. Assuming he may have been on the shelf, how do you think he may have felt? Maybe God had our prophet at another place of training, preparing him for a flaming chariot ride. Our duty is not to be "busy" for God. Our duty is to be clean, filled, ready and willing, expectantly standing on the shelf, ready to be used. We often think that we only have worth when we are busy. God values not our busyness but our readiness.

Life Lessons

Jesus wants you and me to reach our seven-thousand with the message of the quiet whisper.

Consider and discuss: Is God asking you the question, "What are you doing here?

Contemplate the grace, tenderness and love of our Savior God who never gives up on us, even though sometimes we give up on him.

Consider being an encouragement to our Savior God, a "witness" to the world, and experience the loving arms of our Savior.

Ask God right now to reshape your thinking, soften your heart, receive his grace and obey his promptings. Listening is the key! Hear his soft whisper.

CHAPTER 16

Redemption for All

This is Elijah's story, but it seems inextricably woven together with the story of wicked King Ahab. Maybe the Holy Spirit wants us to see the difference between a person dedicated to God and one dedicated to self. All stories end. Before we look at the end of Elijah's story, let's look at the end of King Ahab's. The story of Naboth's vineyard helps cement Ahab's reputation as Israel's most wicked king.

> Sometime later there was an incident involving a vineyard belonging to Naboth the Jezreelite. The vineyard was in

Jezreel, close to the palace of Ahab king of Samaria. Ahab said to Naboth, "Let me have your vineyard to use for a vegetable garden, since it is close to my palace. In exchange I will give you a better vineyard or, if you prefer, I will pay you whatever it is worth." But Naboth replied, "The Lord forbid that I should give you the inheritance of my fathers." So Ahab went home, sullen and angry because Naboth the Jezreelite had said, "I will not give you the inheritance of my fathers." He lay on his bed sulking and refused to eat.

(1 Kings 21:1-4)

This scene takes place as much as five or six years after the "showdown of the gods" on Mount Carmel. Apparently, Ahab felt that he needed a hobby, something to distract him from his troubles. So the mighty king of Israel decided to take up gardening. He decided that the perfect spot for his garden was the property next door that belonged to his neighbor, Naboth. Of course, Ahab didn't see any problem with the fact that someone else owned the perfect spot for his garden; he was the king. *Su casa es mi casa* (your house is my house). I'm sure he thought that his influence was supreme and I imagine he was stunned when Naboth refused. Ahab could not understand why Naboth would refuse because he had so little regard for God's law. Naboth's actions were not prompted by monetary or selfish considerations, but by biblical principles. When God gave the land of Canaan to Israel, He divided it among the twelve tribes. Given human nature, the land (like money) would have tended to accumulate into the hands of the few. And so, the rich would get richer, and the poor would get poorer. God established some very specific laws in Leviticus and Deuteronomy to avoid this. These laws prevented the land from permanently changing hands, outside the family or tribe to which it was allotted. Because of these laws, Naboth knew that he could not sell or trade his land. That is why he responded; "The LORD forbid that I should give you the land of my fathers" (verse 3). The words "the LORD forbid" express not only a strong resolve on Naboth's part, but also a sense of revulsion at the thought of selling (or trading) his land. It was not that Naboth was being unreasonable; this was something he could not do, according to the law; and thus, it was something he would not do, even if the king made him a deal that was tempting. Such principles did not make sense to Ahab. The king, caught completely off guard by Naboth's refusal, went home, crawled into bed, refused to eat, and began to pout.

If Ahab was the most wicked king in Israel's history, I guess Jezebel was his perfect queen.

> Jezebel, his wife said, "Is this how you act as king over Israel? Get up and eat! Cheer up. I'll get you the vineyard of Naboth the Jezreelite." So she wrote letters in Ahab's name, placed his seal on them, and sent them to the elders and nobles who lived in Naboth's city with him. In those letters she wrote: "Proclaim a day of fasting and seat Naboth in a prominent place among the people. But seat two scoundrels opposite him and have them testify that he has cursed both God and the king. Then take him out and stone him to death." So the elders and nobles who lived in Naboth's city did as Jezebel directed in the letters she had written to them. They

proclaimed a fast and seated Naboth in a prominent place among the people. Then two scoundrels came and sat opposite him and brought charges against Naboth before the people, saying, "Naboth has cursed both God and the king." So they took him outside the city and stoned him to death. Then they sent word to Jezebel: "Naboth has been stoned and is dead." As soon as Jezebel heard that Naboth had been stoned to death, she said to Ahab, "Get up and take possession of the vineyard of Naboth the Jezreelite that he refused to sell you. He is no longer alive, but dead." When Ahab heard that Naboth was dead, he got up and went down to take possession of Naboth's vineyard.

(1 Kings 21:7-16)

The hypocrisy of this incident is incredible. It is like a warm-up for the way the Jewish religious leaders will condemn and execute the Lord Jesus on the trumped-up charges of blasphemy (claiming to be God) and insurrection against the king (rebelling against Roman rule). Both travesties of justice were carried out in a way that gave the appearance of religious piety. How

Jezebel must have relished making a mockery of God's laws! Note that a "fast" was called, not a "feast". Fasts were called in times of national disaster, when God's will and word were sought, not when the king wanted to do a little gardening. Both Ahab and Jezebel cared little for the ways of Jehovah. They were each as far from God as a person can get. God's response was to bring in his man, Elijah:

> Then the word of the Lord came to Elijah the Tishbite: "Go down to meet Ahab king of Israel, who rules in Samaria. He is now in Naboth's vineyard, where he has gone to take possession of it. Say to him, 'This is what the Lord says: Have you not murdered a man and seized his property?' Then say to him, 'This is what the Lord says: In the place where dogs licked up Naboth's blood, dogs will lick up your blood — yes, yours!'" Ahab said to Elijah, "So you have found me, my enemy!" "I have found you," he answered, "because you have sold yourself to do evil in the eyes of the Lord I am going to bring disaster on you. I will consume your descendants and cut off from Ahab every last male in Israel — slave or free. I will make your house like

that of Jeroboam son of Nebat and that of Baasha son of Ahijah, because you have provoked me to anger and have caused Israel to sin.' "And also concerning Jezebel the Lord says: 'Dogs will devour Jezebel by the wall of Jezreel.' "Dogs will eat those belonging to Ahab who die in the city, and the birds of the air will feed on those who die in the country." (There was never a man like Ahab, who sold himself to do evil in the eyes of the Lord, urged on by Jezebel his wife. He behaved in the vilest manner by going after idols, like the Amorites the Lord drove out before Israel).

(1 Kings 21:17-26)

Ahab was the worst of the worst and his story is quickly coming to an end. One would expect that judgment was waiting.

When Ahab heard these words, he tore his clothes, put on sackcloth and fasted. He lay in sackcloth and went around meekly. Then the word of the Lord came to Elijah the Tishbite: "Have you noticed how Ahab has humbled himself before me? Because he has humbled himself, I will not bring this disaster in his day.

187

(1 Kings 21:27-29)

Can you believe it? The worst king ever and with one little moment of fear of punishment, one minute of uncharacteristic humbleness and God commutes the sentence.

Apparently, God's default mode is mercy - good news for you and me.

How this challenges our view of God. He is not quick to respond to our personal failure; rather he is quick to forgive and ready to restore as we humble ourselves and admit our sin. No matter the state of your soul today, no matter the blackness of your life, no matter how close you are to the end of your story, God is in the wings of your circumstance, waiting to embrace you with a mercy you have not earned and do not deserve. God is anxiously waiting to dispense kindness; we only need to turn to him.

Life Lessons

Apparently, God's default mode is mercy - good news for you and me.

Consider and discuss: How has God's mercy overwhelmed you and given you hope to start again?

How do we keep from thinking the mercy of God is a license to sin, from thinking God will always forgive, from thinking, "I'll just make my own selfish choices for the day and come back to him at the end of the day for forgiveness?"

What do we miss out on when we aren't moment-by-moment obedient to the still small voice of a merciful and kind God?

CHAPTER 17

A Legacy of Power

Elijah makes several short appearances and eventually arrives at the end of his days on earth but we can't consider the end of Elijah's days without introducing his successor, Elisha. Elisha's life was not only an extension of Elijah's, but as we will see his life was also representative of ours.

> When the LORD was about to take Elijah up to heaven in a whirlwind, Elijah and Elisha were on their way from Gilgal. Elijah said to Elisha, "Stay here; the

LORD has sent me to Bethel." But Elisha said, "As surely as the LORD lives and as you live, I will not leave you." So they went down to Bethel. The company of the prophets at Bethel came out to Elisha and asked, "Do you know that the LORD is going to take your master from you today?" "Yes, I know," Elisha replied, "but do not speak of it." Then Elijah said to him, "Stay here, Elisha; the LORD has sent me to Jericho." And he replied, "As surely as the LORD lives and as you live, I will not leave you." So they went to Jericho. The company of the prophets at Jericho went up to Elisha and asked him, "Do you know that the LORD is going to take your master from you today?" "Yes, I know," he replied, "but do not speak of it." Then Elijah said to him, "Stay here; the LORD has sent me to the Jordan." And he replied, "As surely as the LORD lives and as you live, I will not leave you." So, the two of them walked on. Fifty men of the company of the prophets went and stood at a distance, facing the place where Elijah and Elisha had stopped at the Jordan. Elijah took his cloak, rolled it up and struck the water with it. The water divided to the right and to the left, and the two of them crossed over on dry ground.

(2 Kings 2:1-8)

Was the power in the cloak? Was the power in Elijah? Was the power in God? If the power was in God, then does that mean that we can do mighty works as Elijah did? Imagine the two men on their way to an appointment with Jehovah. God made his will known to Elijah. He had marked his path. Now there was an obstacle in that path. The natural laws that regulate the universe kept the Jordan river always flowing downward, but Elijah was in touch with a higher law, the law of faith. Elijah knew that the path God had for him was beyond the Jordan, and yet there was no clear way to cross. Striking the water with his cloak was just an outward sign of his belief, bringing the power of God to bear on the rushing river.

What do we do when God has given us clear directions. He has given us a clear path to follow. And then suddenly we find ourselves face to face with an immovable barrier to that path. What do we do when that inward prompting points us on, but the Jordan rushes before us? Now is the time for faith. Step down the bank.

Advance and the waters of difficulty will part before you, because where God's finger points, his hand will make a way.

This is the way God means it to be for his people. We aren't to live in the realm of the do-able. We are children of the Most High God. He puts impossible obstacles in front of us to bless us, not hinder us. I wonder how many were following Elijah and watched from a distance that day. "So the world will know that the Lord, he is God."

> When they had crossed, Elijah said to Elisha, "Tell me, what can I do for you before I am taken from you?" "Let me inherit a double portion of your spirit," Elisha replied. "You have asked a difficult thing," Elijah said, "yet if you see me when I am taken from you, it will be yours-- otherwise not." As they were walking along and talking together, suddenly a chariot of fire and horses of fire appeared and separated the two of them, and Elijah went up to heaven in a whirlwind. Elisha saw this and cried out, "My father! My father! The chariots and horsemen of Israel!" And Elisha saw him

no more. Then he took hold of his own clothes and tore them apart. He picked up the cloak that had fallen from Elijah and went back and stood on the bank of the Jordan. Then he took the cloak that had fallen from him and struck the water with it. "Where now is the LORD, the God of Elijah?" he asked. When he struck the water, it divided to the right and to the left, and he crossed over.

(2 Kings 2:9-14)

Does Elisha seem as confident as Elijah? Do you think he was sure? I think he was tentative. God built his confidence with this little event and it seems he never doubted again. Sometimes faith requires a leap! Elisha wanted a double portion of Elijah's power. What would that be like? What kind of power would that be? The Apostle Paul wanted that kind of power as well:

I want to know Christ and the power of his resurrection and the fellowship of sharing in his sufferings, becoming like him in his death.

(Phil. 3:10)

Both Elijah and the Apostle Paul prayed for and received the "Power of the

195

Resurrection." Wow! Is it possible that we could have the same incredible resurrection power that God exercised when he raised his son from the dead? Paul tells us in Ephesians that we already have it, but Paul's concern is that we are not aware of what we have already received:

> I pray also that the eyes of your heart may be enlightened in order that you may know the hope to which he has called you, the riches of his glorious inheritance in the saints, and his incomparably great power for us who believe. That power is like the working of his mighty strength, which he exerted in Christ when he raised him from the dead and seated him at his right hand in the heavenly realms.
>
> (Eph. 1:18-20)

Paul prays that the eyes of our hearts will be opened so we will see that we already have it.

What is resurrection power? It's the power of life over death. Elisha's ministry is a great picture of this power. Except for Jesus, Elisha performed more miracles than any other man in the Bible, and the common thread running through these miracles is resurrection power. Read 2 Kings chapters 2-6 and watch for the many miracles performed by Elisha and how each one typifies the power of life over death. Even in death, Elisha demonstrated God's resurrection power.

A post mortem on Elisha's life:

> Elisha died and was buried. Now Moabite raiders used to enter the country every spring. Once while some Israelites were burying a man, suddenly they saw a band of raiders; so they threw the man's body into Elisha's tomb. When the body touched Elisha's bones, the man came to life and stood up on his feet.
>
> (2 Kings 13:20-21)

Talk about resurrection power!

Okay, so why are we talking about Elisha, in the middle of a book about Elijah? It's because we started this journey together to find the secret to laying hold of God's power for living, and God's power to proclaim the gospel. Do you want this kind of power in your life? If you do, then you have to look closely at Elisha, Elijah's prodigy; he represents you in the story. You see this resurrection power can't be caught, bought or taught. It is transferred from the master to the servant. Elijah was Elisha's master.

Consider the parallelism between the lives of Elijah and Jesus. Elijah is a type-parallel of Christ. Elijah crossed the Jordan; Jesus died on the cross. Elijah and Jesus both ascended to heaven. Elijah sent down his mantle of power to his servant while Jesus sent down the Holy Spirit to his servants. As Elijah was Elisha's master, so Jesus is our master. Elisha received power from Elijah; we receive it from Jesus through his Holy Spirit.

So what is the bottom line? How can you and I receive the power of the resurrection? In the story, Elisha represents us. We receive power the way he did.

Three Steps to resurrection power:

First, we must give all to God.

> So Elijah went from there and found Elisha, son of Shaphat. He was plowing with twelve yoke of oxen, and he himself was driving the twelfth pair. Elijah went up to him and threw his cloak around

him. Elisha then left his oxen and ran after Elijah. "Let me kiss my father and mother good-by," he said, "and then I will come with you." "Go back," Elijah replied. "What have I done to you?" So Elisha left him and went back. He took his yoke of oxen and slaughtered them. He burned the plowing equipment to cook the meat and gave it to the people, and they ate. Then he set out to follow Elijah and became his attendant.

(1 Kings 19:19-21)

Elisha slaughtered the oxen and burned his plowing equipment. There was no turning back.

Second, to receive resurrection power we must die to our own hopes, desires, and plans. Today, many have cheapened what it is to be filled with the power of the Holy Spirit. To be filled with God's Spirit, it is necessary to cross the Jordan with our master. The Jordan River generally typifies death in scripture, but when Elisha crossed the river, he didn't die, he received power. For us, the Jordan typifies our union with Christ in His death. What does it mean to enter into Christ's death? Our union with

Christ into his death means doing what he did. We join him in saying to our father, "… yet not my will, but yours be done" (Luke 22:42)."

The third step to resurrection power is to exercise faith for the blessing. "As surely as the LORD lives and as you live, I will not leave you." If you want to live in the power of the resurrection, don't give up until you have it. Ask for it. It's simple. It's not easy, but it's simple. God is yearning to fill you with his Spirit; expect him to do it. Look at the results for Elisha:

> When they had crossed, Elijah said to Elisha, "Tell me, what can I do for you before I am taken from you?" "Let me inherit a double portion of your spirit," Elisha replied.
>
> (2 Kings 2:9)

Elijah didn't ask Elisha what he could do for him until after they had crossed the river. The river is the final barrier to God's blessing.

The Jordan signifies dying to our own self will and living in the will of the Master. What is not possible for our Master to give us on one side of the Jordan becomes possible on the other.

Life Lessons

Advance and the waters of difficulty will part before you, because where God's finger points, his hand will make a way.

Consider and discuss: Has God given you a dream but you see no possible way that you can possibly fulfill that dream. The fact that the dream is an impossibility is a sure sign that it is from God. Sometimes faith requires a leap. What first step can you take today to tell the Lord that you believe him for his dream?

A God-consciousness will cost you something in your daily decisions, but will gain you a life-time of wealth and wisdom. You truly do not know your strength until you are asked to pick up something in His strength. What excites you most about your next adventure with God?

ABOUT THE AUTHOR

Bob Saffrin lives in Minneapolis, Minnesota with his wife, Barb, and their beagle, Rocky. They have two children and four grandchildren. Bob has been teaching and preaching the Bible for more than thirty-five years. You can reach ˌBob at bobsaffrin@gmail.com or visit his blog at bobsaffrin.com.

OTHER BOOKS BY BOB SAFFRIN

Moses, Steps to a Life of Faith

This book traces some of the significant events of Moses' life showing how God used an ordinary man and shaped the events of his life to bring him to the place where he could be mightily used to accomplish God's purposes. This book is about how God built faith into a man. God is a dreamer. One day he had a dream and then he thought to himself, "Who will I get to fulfill this dream?" And then he made you. He created you to fulfill a dream. You are made for a purpose. This book is about knowing God's dream for your life and believing him to accomplish it in you. This could be the most exciting thing that's ever happened to you. To enter into God's plan for your life is to become the person he made you to be and to finally find the fulfillment and joy that you have been seeking your whole life.

Psalm 23, Help for Lost Lambs

Is there a way of surviving life in our time? So many lives today are troubled, perplexed, stressed and anxious. With all of the threats that are on our body and soul, Is there a way that we can survive without a scratch? There is! The book of Psalms is the answer.
This little book is about the most famous of all the Psalms. Psalm 23 is God's promise that when we find ourselves in trouble he will be with us and he will bring us through it. Read

204

Psalm 23 all over again as if for the very first time.

How to Sleep Like a Baby,

A Meditation on Psalm 3

The 21st century is the age of insomnia. The stresses of life have so multiplied in these times that sleeplessness has become truly epidemic. Check out the bookstore. There are hundreds of books to help you manage the pressure of life and there is more than books. They have DVD's reproducing sounds of forests, oceans, birds and rainfall. They have yoga and eastern mysticism, not to mention stress balls, stress beads, and body rollers that you roll up-and-down your head and back to relieve stress! What does that tell us? I think it tells us that many people in our society, and Christians are not exempt, find it hard to cope with the anxieties of life. It's no wonder we can't sleep. None of us are immune to stressful, anxious days and fretful days can lead to sleepless nights. "How to Sleep Like a Baby" is a meditation on Psalm 3. It is God's prescription for those nights when your mind won't stop thinking about the struggles of the day.

All available at Amazon.com and other book retailers

Made in the USA
Lexington, KY
21 October 2013